THIS BOOK IS FOR Y(

- you have ever wondered what it would be like to visit Jerusalem;

- you would like to know more about the Christian churches in Jerusalem in all their amazing variety;

- you have visited Jerusalem and would like to compare notes;

- you are tired of newspaper headlines about Israel and the Palestinian Territories and would like to get a feel for ordinary life in Jerusalem;

- you are interested in the history of Jerusalem and how we got to be where we are, (the appendices aim to help in this);

- you want to hear some good news about how the Christian churches in Jerusalem are committing themselves to unity;

- you want to be constantly surprised and occasionally shocked;

- you are confused about the rights and wrongs of the situation in Israel and the Palestinian Territories. I hope that after reading this book you will still be confused, but at a deeper level!

Published by
Filament Publishing Ltd
16, Croydon Road,
Beddington, Croydon,
Surrey CR0 4PA
+44(0)20 8688 2598
www.filamentpublishing.com

A Week of Prayer in Jerusalem
by Rev Andy Roland

Map of Jerusalem by Daniel Gould

ISBN 978-1-912256-44-0

Printed by IngramSpark UK

DEDICATION

This book is dedicated to all Israeli and Palestinian

bridge-builders and peacemakers

and to the "Living Stones"

who maintain a Christian presence in the Holy Land

ANDY ROLAND

Andy's interest in Israel was sparked by an article in the Observer newspaper in August 1963 which said anyone could volunteer to take part in a massive archaeological dig at Masada, Herod's fortress-palace by the Dead Sea. Andy went out for a fortnight, and has been back six times since, in 1976, 1990, 1996, 2012, 2015 and 2017.

Having a German Jewish father and a Christian mother, and having studied history at Oxford, his interest in the Holy Land came naturally. His Christian faith led equally naturally to study of the Bible, particularly the links between the Old Testament and the New Testament. He read theology at Durham University and in 1984 was ordained as deacon then priest in the Church of England. He spent 31 years in parishes in south London, and co-led a parish pilgrimage to Israel in 1996.

Since retiring in 2015 he has become engrossed in writing. In April 2017 he published "Bible in Brief", a six month exploration of the Bible with an accompanying website www.bibleinbrief.org; "Discovering Psalms as Prayer", drawing on his experience in South India; and "The Book of Job for Public Performance", with a foreword by Rowan Williams, former Archbishop of Canterbury. He is developing another book about his former parish in south London.

He has an innate curiosity which loves questions rather than quick answers and values journeying over arrival. Come and explore Jerusalem with him!

WHAT OTHERS SAY

"The author of this fascinating book leads the reader into a multi-level experience of the Holy City. With the Week of Prayer for Christian Unity as entry point, Jerusalem's complex history, politics and global symbolic significance are opened up: it is an invitation to understand and empathise with Jerusalem dwellers - but also to journey as pilgrims with deeper understanding and commitment to a just peace."

Mary Grey, Chair of Living Stones oh the Holy Land Trust

"Whether you have only thought of making a pilgrimage to Jerusalem or have already visited this unique city and its various churches, this book provides a company of another traveller, who is fascinated by the diversity and complexity of life and history of Jerusalem.

"Through his easy to read travel diary, Andrew Roland gives us a colourful collage of ordinary and extraordinary encounters with Jerusalemites, places and events. Aware of conflicts and contrasts, as well as human interconnectedness, he joined with the different churches celebrating the Week of Prayer for Christian Unity in the city, from which they all trace their origins."

Rev Eliza Zikmane, Lutheran minister, City of London

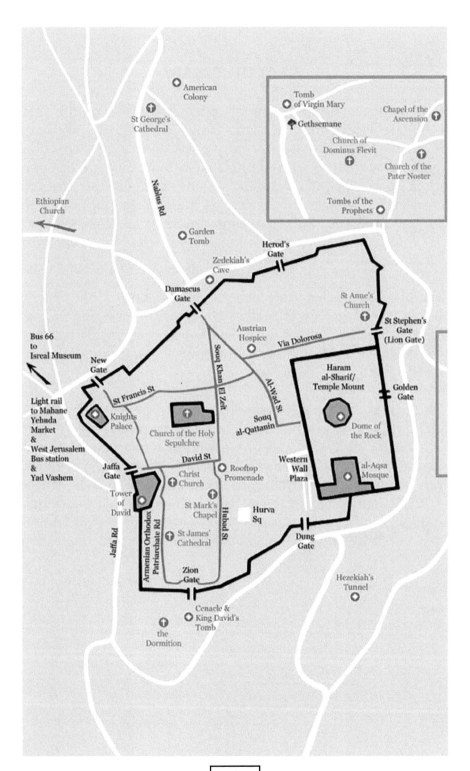

American
Colony

St George's
Cathedral

Tomb
of Virgin Mary

Chapel of the
Ascension

Gethsemane

Church of
Dominus Flevit

Church of the
Pater Noster

Tombs of the
Prophets

Ethiopian
Church

Nablus Rd

Garden
Tomb

Herod's
Gate

Zedekiah's
Cave

Damascus
Gate

St Anne's
Church

Bus 66
to
Isreal Museum

New
Gate

Austrian
Hospice

Via Dolorosa

St Stephen's
Gate
(Lion Gate)

Souq Khan El Zeit

Al-Wad St

Haram
al-Sharif/
Temple Mount

Golden
Gate

Light rail
to Mahane
Yehuda
Market
&
West Jerusalem
Bus station
&
Yad Vashem

St Francis St

Knights
Palace

Church of the Holy
Sepulchre

Souq
al-Qattanin

Dome of
the Rock

David St

Jaffa
Gate

Christ
Church

Rooftop
Promenade

Western
Wall
Plaza

al-Aqsa
Mosque

Tower
of
David

St Mark's
Chapel

Hurva
Sq

Jaffa Rd

Armenian Orthodox
Patriarchate Rd

Habad St

St James'
Cathedral

Dung
Gate

Zion
Gate

Hezekiah's
Tunnel

Cenacle &
King David's
Tomb

the
Dormition

TABLE OF CONTENTS

APPENDICES

INTRODUCTION

Welcome to Jerusalem!

The city with 3,000 years of history and the focus of three major faiths, Judaism, Christianity and Islam.

People often come as part of a pilgrim group. I like to go round places on my own. I may not see everything, but I do have my own unique experiences and encounters.

"A Week of Prayer in Jerusalem" is the travel diary of my week in Jerusalem when I came to take part in the Week of Prayer for Christian Unity. I have now been to Jerusalem seven times in all, the last three during the Week of Prayer. In England we used to try to have just one unity service in the week. In Jerusalem they take it much more seriously, and there is a unity service at 5.00 every day, except on Thursday when it is 4.00. This visit followed on from two previous pilgrimages which I made with Living Stones. Living Stones Holy Land Trust aims to tell people about the situation of Christians in the Holy Land, and to support them where possible.

This time I wanted to put on record my experience of the Week of Prayer in Jerusalem and to re-acquaint myself with the city in all its religious, social and political complexity.

Come and explore Jerusalem with me. I hope that in consequence you will feel able to make your own journey there.

THE TRAVELLERS

ANDY ROLAND

 I was born in 1945 and grew up in Coventry and Rugby. My father was secular German Jewish and my mother a Quaker Anglican. I studied history at Oxford University and after a short spell teaching went into personnel management. I was ordained in 1984 and served as priest in south London, 21 years in the parish of Hackbridge and Beddington Corner, and marrying in 2000. I have now visited Israel seven times.

1963 I worked as a volunteer for two weeks on the archaeological site of Masada, spending Christmas in West Jerusalem, then joining my parents for a visit to Galilee and Tel Aviv. At Masada the Israeli archaeologist in charge of our section constantly wore a red-checked Arab scarf; he had taken it from a Jordanian soldier he had killed in 1948. He also told me a story of the fight against the Britisn Mandate pre-1948. A British officer had interrogated two young Jewish fighters so brutally that the girl died. So they sent him a book in the post. When he opened it, it blew his head off. In Jerusalem I met an old friend of my father's who worked to help Soviet Jews settle into the very different society of Israel. I said to him that I thought that modern Israelis had lost that wonderful Jewish sense of humour I had grown up with. He paused reflectively, then said, *"Yes, it's hard to have a sense of humour as a victorious military power."*

1975 I came on a pilgrimage organised by Imperial College chaplaincy, where I worked at the time. It included staying at various youth hostels and a schoolroom in Bethlehem. I met some human rights workers in Nazareth and learnt about some of the legal restrictions which faced Israeli Arabs. We celebrated Holy Week in Jerusalem, a wonderful experience.

1990 I visited Galilee with a friend from Tel Aviv I had first met at the church in Streatham where I had worked. A highlight was staying in the village of Ibillin, Galilee and meeting Fr. Elias Chacour. I spent some time in Jerusalem meeting some interesting people, including the "Women in Black". These are a group of women who spend one hour every Friday lunchtime standing in silence to protest against Israel's oppressive policy to Palestinians. No posters, or placards, simply an hour's silence. The abuse that got hurled at them had to be seen to be believed. I got on well with a Reform rabbi and said to him that I found the best books about Jesus were written by Jews, (I was thinking of Geza Vermes and others). *"Yes"*, he replied, *"the New Testament"*.

1996 I co-led a pilgrimage with Rev Selwyn Tillett from our adjoining churches in Beddington, South London. We went from Tel Aviv and Yafo to stay at a wonderful Anglican hospice in Nazareth, ending up in Jerusalem. While there, there was the first in a series of bomb attacks on "soft" Israeli targets, a cafe in Tel Aviv. We could see how everyone, Israeli soldiers and Palestinians alike, shared the same fear and dread.

2012 When the Separation Wall started being built, I felt I could not go back again. But Jo Simister was a member of my parish and Vice Chair of Living Stones, an organisation aiming to support Christians in Israel and the Palestinian territories. In 2012 Linda and I went with her on a "Living Stones" pilgrimage during the Week of Prayer for Christian Unity. This gave equal exposure to the holy sites, including the place of Jesus' baptism in the Jordan, as well as to Palestinian projects like the Princess Basma Centre for Disabled Children, the Augusta Victoria Hospital and the Quaker school in Ramallah,

West Bank. Linda and I had a couple of days before and after in Jerusalem and Nazareth, and we also visited Masada, Herod's fortress-palace by the Dead Sea.

2015 I went on another Living Stones pilgrimage during the Week of Prayer for Christian Unity, this time visiting Hebron as well.

JO SIMISTER

Jo was born in Walsall and drifted into teaching, particularly art and music, printing and pottery, gaining her qualification at the West Midlands College, part of Birmingham University. What she most enjoyed was maternity leave supply teaching children in hospital.

Jo's curiosity about the cultural background of the bible was aroused when the 'Bible Come to Life' exhibition came to her deanery in Tamworth. She helped with finding volunteers to wear the beautiful costumes for the tableaux each evening, and one thing stuck in her mind: that in order to understand Abraham you have to know Bedouin culture.

Shortly after, Jo became Deputy Warden of the Methodist International House in Bayswater in London, an experience which quickly removed any shyness around communicating in the simplest English – and was a baptism of fire in international relations as nearly all the one hundred students had to share rooms with strangers; *"The trick is to have a language or a faith in common".*

In 1986, she said, *"I'd quite like to go to the Holy Land",* and a friend said, *"Choose what you want to do, and I'll share a room with you."*

A group of seven went on a two week cultural trip starting in Jordan and travelling to Nablus, Nazareth, Bethlehem, East Jerusalem, Ein Gedi, Eilat, St Catherine's Monastery in Sinai, and back via Aqaba and Petra. It changed the direction of her life. She now wanted to work in Palestine but 'as a worker who happens to be Christian, not as a Christian'. It took nine months, but in the end, through the Quaker Middle East Placement Programme she started work at the Princess Basma Centre for Disabled Children on the Mount of Olives. Mrs Majaj the Director had just started a school there as well, and Jo was her first PA.

As Jo's two-year placement came to end, Save the Children Fund's Middle East Regional Advisor asked if she would work with Lesley, who was busy setting up a degree course in physiotherapy at Bethlehem University, to help with admin and overseeing the scholarships for the students – and eventually teaching some courses on disability awareness and course planning.

Jo returned to the UK in 1997 and I first met her when she moved to my parish. She had joined Living Stones and was helping with their administration. She had known of it before, when living in Jerusalem, and been impressed with the founder, theologian Revd Dr Michael Prior. In 2012 she and Lesley led the first Living Stones pilgrimage to Israel and the Occupied Palestinian Territories and they hope it will be able to continue every year.

LESLEY DAWSON

Lesley qualified as a physiotherapist in 1963, and worked at Bradford, Bethlehem and Brighton, ending up with a PhD in Education. She headed up a team setting up a degree course for physiotherapists at Bethlehem University in 1988, funded by Save The Children Fund. She came intending to stay four years and actually stayed eleven. This included three months in Gaza as an Educational Consultant. When the Intifada started in December 1987, Israel closed all schools and universities in the West Bank and Gaza, so for the first few years the teaching took place in the Notre Dame Teaching Centre in Jerusalem.

After 1999 she lived at Eastbourne and taught at the University of Brighton, retiring in 2007. She still carries out programme evaluations abroad. She joined Living Stones in 2000 and has gone back with Living Stones for the last five years, keeping contact with former students.

SATURDAY 21st JANUARY

ARRIVAL

Jo, Lesley and I met up without difficulty at Luton, flying by Easyjet. Security checks and flight were uneventful. I sat next to a young Jewish couple from Highgate, north London, Jake and Charlotte, who were going out partly as holiday at the father's house at Herzliya 50 metres from the beach. (You need some serious money to have that). He was also meeting up with his brother in Tel Aviv about a charity their family had set up to help homeless people in Tel Aviv. There is homelessness there as in any other big city. I asked if the settlements on the West Bank were a way of helping Israel's housing crisis. They said no, the settlements are more strategic and political. Most homelessness was caused by families splitting up, typically young people from ultra-religious families, especially if they were gay. Gay people and secular Israelis often fly over to Cyprus to get married. (This was what two friends of mine had done). They also commented on how the Jerusalem municipality was not good at providing basic services to the Muslim and Christian quarters of East Jerusalem, such as water and rubbish collection.

As we came into Israeli air space we could see the sharp line between the lights of Tel Aviv and the dark of the Mediterranean. We landed at Ben Gurion airport and went through to departure without incident. The airport was named after the first Prime Minister of Israel in 1973. David ben Gurion, 1886-1973, was Prime Minister 1948-1954 and 1955-1963. I remember that when I first landed there in 1963, it was called Lod airport, after the Israeli name for Lydda, a Palestinian village whose inhabitants were forced into the refugee camps of Gaza in 1948. It had been the place where St Peter prayed for a paralysed man called Aeneas, (Acts 9.32-35). It was also the birthplace of St George, a Christian soldier who was martyred under the persecution of the Roman Emperor Diocletian in 303. He is the patron saint of Portugal, Catalonia, Romania, and of course England. The airport lies on the outskirts of the city of Lod, which has about 70,000 inhabitants, just over 1,000 being Arabs who are still there after the remainder had been expelled.

 As we left the airport we saw an impressive sculpture by Salvador Dali of the menorah, the seven-branched candlestick that was central to the worship of the Temple in Jerusalem. The arch of Titus in Rome shows the menorah being carried by the victorious Roman troops after the crushing of the Jewish revolt in 68 C.E. The feast of Hanukkah in December commemorates the miracle of the lighting of the Menorah after the Maccabees had defeated the Seleucid kingdom based in Persia, and had re-consecrated the Temple after the king's attempt to eradicate the Jewish faith in 168 B.C. You can read about it in some Bibles which include later books written in Greek, called the Apocrypha. The story is in 1 Maccabees 4.36-59.

We were picked up in a car by Bassam, a Christian Palestinian and an old friend of Jo and Lesley. His surname means the old eastern function of "dragoman", a mixture of interpreter, guide and fixer, very appropriate. He brought us to our hotel, the Knight's Palace, inside the walls of the Old City in the Roman Catholic district, the Latin Patriarchate. The rooms were clean and basic, with electric air conditioning which also provided heating - essential in Jerusalem in January. The floors are

stone, as always in a hot climate, but in January they are very chilly. When Linda and I came in 2012 we could not get the heater to work and spent the coldest night of our lives! So don't forget slippers and a hot water bottle!

We arrived too late for food, but Bassam arranged for us to walk a couple of hundred yards to the Gloria Hotel, who fed us very well indeed. Palestinian hotel meals all follow the same self-service pattern - soup, a splendid salad selection, a main meat course and some sweet pastry or fruit. It also had a better bar than the Knight's Palace. Lesley asked if the two hotels were owned by same company. "Owned by the same family", Bassam replied laconically.

SUNDAY 22nd JANUARY

A CHRISTIAN SABBATH

Breakfast was a buffet style including cereals, porridge, salads, cold meats and a hot dish like scrambled eggs. Tea and coffee was served by the staff in small cups, very small compared with the mugs I use at home. But the waiters were always quick to refill my cup. Note: If you are a vegetarian, be prepared to eat lots of hummus and omelettes.

About 8.30 I wandered down to the Church of the Holy Sepulchre, down St Francis Street, up Christian Quarter Road, then slipped down St Helena Street to the square in front of the fairly unimpressive entrance to the holiest church in Christendom. Many Western Christians find Holy Sepulchre hard to take. It is dark, and usually full of scaffolding and pilgrims of every continent doing their own thing, lighting candles, kissing stones, taking flash photos. The various ancient churches are jealous of their own bits of territory. Indeed the only way that the

keys of the church could be handled peacefully is by a Muslim family. But over the years I have found it a very special place, more like a small town with a variety of chapels than a neat well-organised Anglican cathedral.

CHURCH OF THE HOLY SEPULCHRE
A BRIEF HISTORY

The history is complicated. Early on, Jewish Christians venerated the place where Jesus died and the nearby rock-tomb which was the site of this resurrection. When the Emperor Hadrian razed the city after the revolt of Bar-Kochba in 132-136 AD, he deliberately created a new pagan city in which Jews were not allowed. The tradition is that he built a shrine and temple to Venus over the empty tomb and Golgotha. After Christianity became a legal religion in 316 and received imperial favour, the temple was demolished and a splendid new church built with a kind of plaza incorporating both the rocky column of Calvary and the rock tomb of Jesus. It was begun in 326 and completed nine years later. It was damaged during the Persian invasion of 614 but repaired when the Byzantines recaptured it. However, in 638 the Arab armies, inspired by their Muslim faith, captured Jerusalem along with Palestine, Syria and in 640 Egypt.

The Patriarch, who had sent the holy relics to Constantinople for safe keeping, invited Caliph Omar to pray in the church, but the Caliph refused, saying that if he did so, his followers might want to turn the church into a mosque. For the first 100 years there was no attempt at converting the local population to Islam. Thereafter conversions happened, though in 1200 there was still a Christian majority in Egypt. In 1922 73,000 or 10.8% of Palestinians were Christian; in 1946 the figure was about 9%. Now it is only 1%. Life under Islam was reasonably tolerant as second-class citizens, except in the middle years of Caliph al-Hakim of Egypt. He reigned from 996 (at the age of 11) till 1021. In 1009 he started a campaign against churches and synagogues during which he had Constantine's Church of the Holy Sepulchre destroyed, chipping away at the rock which contained the tomb of Jesus until the site was levelled. He came to believe that he was the Mahdi, the prophesied redeemer of Islam. He started withdrawing for nights of meditation. One night in 1021 he rode out and nothing was ever seen of him again, apart from his donkey and a blood-stained coat. The Druze community, centred round Lebanon, Syria and Israel, are a Muslim sect who believe that Hakim did not die but will return one day.

Restoration of the church began straightaway but proceeded slowly. Twenty years later the Byzantine emperor provided funds for some rebuilding, but a large part was abandoned. After the brutal capture of Jerusalem by the Crusaders in 1099, the new Frankish regime rebuilt the church and the rotunda around the tomb. The Knights Templar built round churches in Europe as a reminder of the church in Jerusalem. You can see examples in the Temple Church in London and in the Round Church in Cambridge. After the defeat of the Crusaders by Salah-ed-Din (Saladin) in 1189 one of the main entrances was walled up, and the keys of the church, with responsibility for opening and closing the church, was given to a local Muslim family, the Nusseibehs, who have been responsible every since. This was because the various churches who had chapels in the Church, (Franciscans and Orthodox of various nationalities), could not agree among themselves how it should be done. Little change happened until a disastrous fire in 1808, and then an earthquake in 1927 caused extensive damage.

The disagreements between the various churches meant that repairs did not get under way until 1959. I have always known the church to be covered in scaffolding until 2014, when it was finally clear as a result of UNESCO funding.

VISITING THE CHURCH OF THE HOLY SEPULCHRE

When I entered the church, I made a circuit anti-clockwise and saw at once that the scaffolding was back. Walking behind it at the east end I discovered a small chapel which was used by the Syrian Orthodox Church, the chapel of St Nicodemus. There is a small doorway here which leads to a number of first century rock tombs - clearly the site of some sort of cemetery.

(I have had a soft spot for the Syrian Orthodox church ever since I started using part of their morning prayer service in my prayers after visiting a Christian Ashram in south India in 1983. My book "Discovering Psalms as Prayer" tells the story). I said my own Syrian Orthodox morning prayers, in English, while the preparatory prayers before the liturgy were being said by a priest, and an elderly woman. The liturgy started when a surprisingly young bishop arrived. I could understand nothing so I left after a bit to witness the end of a Coptic service held in a kind of plastic tent beneath the scaffolding surrounding the Chapel of the Resurrection. In the main nave of the church the Greek Orthodox service was just beginning. In a small side space with an altar I saw a Greek Orthodox priest standing motionless for over half an hour, while he read the morning prayers from his service book. Chapels continue down into the bowels of the earth - actually an old Roman cistern, where Constantine's wife

Helena discovered the true cross buried. She actually discovered three crosses, but reckoned that the only one that got people healed was the Real Thing. Pilgrims used to bite fragments off while kissing it devoutly till not much was left. Erasmus in the sixteenth century said that there were enough pieces of the true cross in churches in Europe to build a ship! However, it is a mysterious space with an atmosphere that makes prayer almost imperative. I then went to the Chapel of Calvary, the actual spot, probably, where Jesus was crucified.

It consists of two elaborate chapels, both quite small. The first one you come to is owned by the Franciscans with lots of paintings and candles.

It commemorates the moment when Jesus was stripped of his clothes. The second, the Greek Orthodox one, full of chandeliers and candles, centres on the altar over the hole in the bare rock where the cross stood, pilgrims taking it in turns to kneel down and kiss the rough stone. There was a group of pilgrims from Ethiopia, dressed in white, praying and taking photos with their laptops, and I did the same with my small camera. Then down steep steps to ground level where there was a surprisingly short queue to enter the Chapel of the Resurrection.

A small doorway is guarded by two attendants who make sure that people do not stay too long in the chapel. It was upsetting to see a woman being hurried out of the chapel quite roughly with the attendants saying, *"Quickly, quickly!"* You duck down beneath a low stone arch and come into a tiny vestibule,where you wait to take your turn in the actual tomb itself, a small oblong space with a 6 foot marble slab marking where the body of Jesus would have lain. There is just room for three

people to kneel side by side and just enough time to say the Lord's Prayer. On one of my previous visits I got a tap on the shoulder to indicate that my time was up, and as I left the attendant said, *"God is outside as well,"* to which I thought, *"That's true."*

Opposite the tomb is the main body of the church. A Greek Orthodox service was about to start. The wealth of new decoration contrasts with the down-at-heel look of other parts. But there is a problem. The Greek Orthodox keep a tight hold on many of the religious sites, and bishops and priests are almost exclusively Greek, not Palestinian. Other churches are led by local Palestinian clergy. It is one of the strengths of the Uniate Churches, i.e Orthodox churches in communion with Rome.

I made my way to the Ethiopian monastery. This is one of the oddest corners of Jerusalem. In the early 20th century the Ethiopian Church became independent from the Coptic, Egyptian church. As a result the Ethiopian monks were kicked out of the Coptic Monastery, not very Christian, and made their home in the ruined Crusader cloisters on the actual roof of the Church of the Holy Sepulchre. It was originally shared between the Ethiopians and the Copts, but in 1970, while the Coptic monks were away celebrating Easter, the Ethiopians changed the locks! Also not very Christian.

This was my route: Out into the courtyard and up to Christian

Quarter Road; turning right down Aqabat al Khanqah St. There I met a rubbish collection truck which is not only narrow enough to get through the souks, but actually goes up and down steps! Then right at the crossroads down Souk Khan al-Zeit and after a few yards I turned right up some wide steps by a juice stand turning left, right and right. In front is the entrance to the Coptic Church, Just in front are two doorways. The one on the right leads to an ancient cistern. The one on the left leads to the Ethiopian monastery.

I first discovered this in 1986. It was a quiet, peaceful square, with some of the monks' washing hanging out to dry. The dome in the middle of the courtyard is directly over the chapel of St Helena, where stairs go down into the bowels of the earth. I tried to speak to a thin elderly monk who was selling icons. He knew no English, but he did sell me a beautiful small icon of Christ the suffering King, and it has been a treasured possession of mine ever since.

It now seems to have become a standard part of pilgrim tours, I am sure to the dismay of the Ethiopian monks who still live there, and now keep themselves very much behind their green shuttered doors and windows. This time my visit coincided with that of a large pilgrim group from Kerala. Kerala is in the south-west of India and has the largest Christian presence of all Indian states, about 25%. Christianity has been in Kerala at least since the 4th century. There are several stone reliefs of the Syrian Orthodox life-giving cross from the 7th-8th centuries. Tradition has it that the first missionary was St Thomas (Doubting Thomas) who was martyred near Chennai/Madras and is buried on a hill outside that city.

We all went through a narrow door through a dusty chapel and down some narrow stairs to the Church of the Holy Sepulchre. I was struck by the portrayal of the Trinity in the chapel: God,

not as an old man in the sky, but as three old men in the sky. Not quite my understanding.
(I wrote a blog "God in 3D" for my website bibleinbrief.org, in which I try to explain what the Trinity means).

A JERUSALEM SUNDAY

Then it was time for church! I had discovered that the Lutheran church, just round the corner from the Church of the Holy Sepulchre, had a service at 10.15. It is an impressive neo-romanesque building in beautiful golden stone with the spire one of the landmarks of the Old City. It was built when German influence was at its height, with the Kaiser supporting the Ottoman empire. When Kaiser Wilhelm II made a state visit to Jerusalem in 1898 to dedicate the new church, the Ottoman authorities demolished a whole section of the wall by Jaffa gate, originally built by Sultan Sulemein the Magnificent between 1537 and 1541, as the Kaiser's cavalcade could not squeeze through Jaffa gate itself. I decided to go to the

Lutherans because I had been learning German for the last year at the Goethe Institut at South Kensington. I was able to understand the reading of John 4.46-54 which was written down, but not much else, including pastor Melanie's sermon. But I did appreciate the end, when all of us, about 35, stood in a circle to receive communion and then held hands for the blessing. All baptised Christians, including children, were invited. Afterwards there were refreshments in the lovely first floor cloisters (originally from the 11th century church of St Mary-la-Latine) - sage tea, no coffee. Sage tea is the winter drink and is reputed to keep colds at bay and be good for sexual function. Mint tea is the summer drink. Not many came to take part, but I chatted with a couple from near Hamburg, a lawyer and a social worker. The husband spoke of his longing for the visible unity of the church, as that would herald the return of Christ.

I wandered back through the Old City towards Jaffa Gate, hoping to pick up a free street map from the Israeli Tourist Office. At the bottom of the Latin Patriarchate Road I was accosted by an Armenian merchant who invited me into his small jewellery workshop. Talk about pushy! He was the most skilful operator I have every come across. Thank goodness I had come out without too much money and without my credit card! (An important precaution in any eastern city).

Nevertheless, after a lecture about the various qualities of the stones and a demonstration of threading them to make a necklace, how to tell the difference between genuine stones and fake Chinese ones (the latter are magnetic), and how he is doing up his grandfather's shop, I succumbed and bought the necklace for Linda. I had intended to get something like that for her anyway. The merchant told me about the illness of his mother Nola, and I prayed for her with him, so he might have sold it to me at a slightly lower price than otherwise. He then asked if I had any other family members. In my reply I mentioned my niece Ali (short for Alison) who had just given birth to a baby daughter. *"I saw your eyes light up! You must give her this!'* And guess what, I did. What a master of psychology!

On leaving, feeling hungry and exhausted, I was accosted by another merchant who asked me to walk into his shop: "Just look!". I said I did not want to do that I said I just wanted something to eat. Quick as a flash, he called a young lad to escort me to a nearby restaurant where I had falafel and salad and mint tea for 60 NIS - a bit over the normal price, but OK.

I then walked wearily back through the steep little market streets to the Damascus Gate, where the Christian Quarter and the Muslim Quarter meet. This is the main gate in the

northern wall of Jerusalem and has been that for at least 2,000 years. The present gateway is part of Suleiman the Magnificent's work of 1537-1541. Below the gateway and to the left is one of the two side arches of the gateway built under the emperor Hadrian (ruled 117-138), and only excavated in 1964-6. Damascus Gate is the entry point into the Palestinian side of East Jerusalem. I walked straight down the Nablus Road, aiming at St George's Anglican Cathedral half a mile away. I passed the Garden Tomb (closed on Sundays) which General Gordon, in 1883, had identified as the site of the crucifixion and empty tomb, especially as his diggings uncovered some ancient rock tombs. A tranquil and beautiful spot, but in my opinion not the real deal. I passed the Syrian Orthodox monastery where the Living Stones pilgrimage had stayed in 2016. Eventually I found my way to the American Colony Hotel where I had arranged to meet Jo and Lesley for tea about 4.00.

Jerusalem is an exhausting place to be around. Those who have been a few times are quick to discover oases of peace and tranquility and good European coffee, for instance, the Austrian Hospice in the Old City, and the American Colony Hotel in East Jerusalem. The roots of the American Colony lie with Horatio Spafford, an American lawyer, and his wife Anna. They were devout Christians, and after the great fire of Chicago of 1881, decided to travel to Europe in 1883, Anna and their three children going first. On the way their liner was hit by an British ship and sank immediately. All three children drowned. On reaching Liverpool, she sent her husband the famous telegram: "Saved alone. What shall I do?" Spafford immediately went out to join her, and when the ship sailed over the spot of the tragedy, he wrote the well-known hymn:

When peace like a river, attendeth my way,
When sorrows like sea billows roll;
Whatever my lot, Thou hast taught me to know,
It is well, it is well, with my soul.
   It is well, (it is well)
   With my soul, (with my soul)
   It is well, it is well, with my soul.

Eight years later he set sail with a dozen adults and three children to build a new life in Jerusalem. They formed a commune and aimed to help all they came across, regardless of religion. Spafford hoped this would speed the second coming of Christ. Spafford died in 1888, but Anna persuaded a large group of Swedes to join them. In 1896 38 Swedish adults and 17 children joined them. The Colony now numbered 150 and moved into the large house of a wealthy Arab landowner. Here they set up a small farm and taught in both Jewish and Muslim schools. The colony finally ceased in the 1950's, and the building became the American Colony Hotel. It still continues its tradition of hospitality and welcome. Indeed, the first meeting between representatives of the Israeli Government and the Palestinian Liberation Organisation

 happened here, which led, in 1993, to the Oslo accords and a brief season of hope.

It is still a great place for afternoon tea, with large cool rooms, leather sofas and hushed waiters. It is only 100 yards from St George's, so that was why it was our meeting place. I got there early and flopped on one of the leather sofas. When Jo and Lesley arrived we had tea and scones. They had been to the Scottish Church in the morning, where they found six old ladies making up the congregation and four ministers!

We got to St George's early to find the cathedral was already full with 150 people in the congregation, and, as happens every year, the need to bring in more chairs and service sheets. St George's Cathedral was consecrated in 1910 and is a cross between a traditional parish church and a small-scale cathedral with cloisters and a close. Inside the cathedral hangs the royal coat-of-arms which decorated the British High Commission up to May 1948, when the British withdrew from Palestine, unable any longer to mediate between Arab terrorism (e.g. the Palestinian Revolt of 1936-39) and Jewish terrorism (e.g. the blowing up of the south wing of the King David Hotel in 1946).

The Cathedral has a mixed Arab and English congregation. There have been Anglican bishops in Jerusalem since 1841; they have all been Palestinian since 1976. Both Bishop Suheili Dawani and Dean Hosam Naoum are Palestinian. But the service was entirely in English. The service began with

the hymn, *"Songs of thankfulness and praise,,,",* We joined in saying part of Psalm 118 and the Magnificat. The readings were Isaiah 53.4-12: *"Surely he has borne our infirmities and carried our diseases, yet we accounted him stricken, struck down by God and afflicted",* and John 15.13-17: *"I am giving you these commands so that you may love one another."*

All the readings are taken from the services for the Week of Prayer prepared by the World Council of Churches, this year by the churches of Latvia.

In his homily Bishop Suheil recounted how he had recently hosted a visit to St George's of a Roman Catholic party, including a Roman Catholic bishop, and how a hundred years ago that would have been completely unthinkable. We then renewed our baptism vows, taking a pinch of salt and lighting a thin candle or taper as a sign of our mission to be salt and light to the world. After the creed, Hosam Naoum, the dean of the cathedral, led a short litany. i.e. a pattern of prayers and responses, e.g.

"O Christ, Savior and Lord,
extend your Church to every place.
Make it a place of welcome
for people of every race and tongue".
The grace of God be with us all."

All the bishops of the various churches stood together at the east end to give the blessing, based on the Beatitudes of Matthew 5.3-12. I noticed that, rather unfortunately, the service booklet had left out the fourth beatitude: "Blessed are those who hunger and thirst after righteousness, for they will be filled", especially as standing up against injustice is central to the cathedral's ministry. Then followed the hymn *"The Church's one foundation,"* which speaks quite realistically of the difficulties facing the worldwide church;

"Though with a scornful wonder
Men see her sore oppressed,
By schisms rent asunder,
By heresies distressed."

The service ended, as usual, with the toccata and fugue in D minor by J S Bach on the organ, which everyone seemed very impressed by. I felt that it sounded a bit weak compared with some churches in England, but of course to have an organ at all in a place where most churches, being Orthodox, have only unaccompanied singing, can sound quite exotic.

Afterwards we were all invited to "a humble reception" at the Pilgrim Guest House, with tea,coffee and biscuits. I met Melanie, the Lutheran pastor, and Poirag (or Patrick), the minister of the Scottish Church, who, when I said I was British, responded pointedly *"I'm Irish."* I chatted to a very interesting Englishman called Joel who was working for the time being in the dean's office. He talked enthusiastically about the Palm Sunday procession the previous year, one of those rare years when western Christians and eastern orthodox Christians celebrate Easter on the same day. He had taken part in the great Palm Sunday procession from the Mount of Olives to the Church of the Holy Sepulchre, and he spoke of the joy that people felt being united together, Catholics, Orthodox and Protestants, Palestinian Christians and Jewish Christians, including a group of Hebrew Catholic Christians who sang and danced in worship along the mile-long route. There is a real possibility that all the churches of Jerusalem might agree on a common date for Easter; the idea is supported by Bartholomew, the Ecumenical Patriarch of Constantinople.

Joel is an architect and had come out to Israel along with his wife Fiona, a Norwegian. She had come out under the auspices of the Norwegian Refugee Council to help provide shelter for Palestinians who had their homes demolished by the Israeli authorities. (The work is too political for it to be undertaken by Norwegian Church Aid). Joel uses his training as an architect to design adequate temporary shelters, particularly in the cold winter months, which they call 'winterising'. The work is carried out by Global Shelter Cluster, which provides emergency shelters all over the world, e.g. in Somalia where 793,000 people have fled their homes because of drought, and in Peru where 8,975 houses have been affected by floods. In the Palestinian territories, in the five months January to May, 335 demolitions have been carried out by the Israeli authorities, affecting 1,594 people, see www.sheltercluster.org.

Then back to the Knights' Palace Hotel, supper and bed.

MONDAY 23rd JANUARY

TO BE A PILGRIM

I met Jo and Lesley at breakfast. They were going to visit Nablus, the second largest city on the West Bank in order to meet up with some of their former physiotherapy graduates. Lesley had tutored them in the degree course she had set up in 1987 at Bethlehem University, and Jo had helped them with the scholarships which would cover their education and link them into eventual work, including at the Princess Basma Centre for Disabled Children. Also at breakfast was their friend

and colleague Bassam who was going to drive them there. Bassam had worked with the United Nations staff in the Occupied Territories and basically knew everyone in Jerusalem and throughout the West Bank. He has three children aged 24 to 29. His youngest daughter is completing an M.A. in Psychology and is a consultant on educational development in Dubai. She would have liked to train as a doctor, but that had proved too complicated. His son is in Düsseldorf, Germany, studying European Affairs and Diplomacy. He wants to become an academic because he wants to be able to speak the truth, and not get caught up in the compromises of politics. Bassam's eldest daughter gained an M.A. in film-making at New York College and would like to make films in the Palestinian Territories, but there are no opportunities there now, so she will probably go back to New York.

My plan was to walk on a mini-pilgrimage from the Mount of Olives to the Armenian Cathedral of St James. I had thought of starting out by taxi, but Jo and Lesley said it is easy to get a bus at the East Jerusalem bus station (the place which General Gordon had thought was the site of Golgotha). So I walked along the narrow streets of the souk, admiring the tiny rubbish vans which trundle up and down. I talked for a while to an elderly cobbler, Nabil, who still works in his grandfather's narrow workshop in Souk Khan el- Z e i t, which has been in the family since 1946.

The souks demonstrate the change in position between Jews and Arabs in the Old City. All of the shops now have t-shirts

and memorabilia designed to appeal to Israelis and Jewish visitors. So different from 20 years ago. Damascus Gate is now quite intimidating, with heavy Israeli army and police presence, and Hasidic Jews ducking fearfully through the gaggles of Palestinian shoppers. Outside Damascus Gate I headed towards the bus station but noticed a sign saying "Zedekiah's Caves". I paid my 10 NIS and went in. It is the most amazing underground quarry, over 300 feet long. it was

used for Herod's Temple and earlier, as well as for the 1540's walls of the City. It is extraordinary that a few thick columns of rock left from the quarrying are all that hold up five city blocks of the Old City!

I had thought I might get the light rail (or tram) from the Damascus Gate, but it veers north rather than south. I was able to find the right bus for the Mount of Olives, number 275 at the East Jerusalem bus station. You can see the cave in the rock face behind it, which made General Gordon believe that that was the true site of Golgotha, the Place of the Skull. My problem was that I did not know when to get off. The Mount of Olives does not have one particular high point, rather, it is a long ridge interrupted by the Separation Wall which divides Bethany off from the rest of Jerusalem. So I got off one stop too late

at the Augusta Victoria Hospital, at the northern end of the ridge. I had visited the Augusta Victoria as part of the two previous Living Stones pilgrimages, so I knew where I was.

Augusta Victoria Hospital is one of the landmarks of Jerusalem, with its 50 metre church tower. It was built between 1907 and 1914 by the wife of Kaiser Wilhelm II as a church and

hospital compound. It has had a chequered history through two world wars and two wars with Israel. It is still one of the most important health facilities for Palestinians, with 161 beds and an advanced centre for cancer treatments. Some of the physiotherapists whom Lesley and Jo had graduated work there, but they always have the anxiety of whether they will get through the Israeli checkpoints in time to get to work. The hospital had planned a residential home for elderly Palestinians who had no other support, an initiative which was supported by the Israeli Ministry of Health, but opposed by the Israeli Interior Ministry. Unfortunately the Interior Ministry won.

There are amazing views of the Russian Orthodox Monastery

spire and of the hills of the West Bank, together with a Jewish settlement. There is also the only all-weather football pitch in the Palestinian areas, one of the few sports facilities available to Palestinian young people. It is a legacy of the British mandate, because the soldiers required somewhere to play soccer. The hospital authorities have to engage in a kind of peaceful resistance to the constant attempts by Israel to take over the hospital grounds. They have to ensure that their land cannot be categorised as unused and therefore vulnerable to being classified as state land and then taken over.

I had a 20 minute walk along the ridge, passing the Makassed Islamic Charitable Hospital (250 beds) and the Princess Basma Centre for Disabled Children to reach my first stop, the Chapel of the Ascension. This is a unique piece of

Jerusalem, inhabiting a sort of quiet no man's land between Christians, Muslims and latterly Jews. It is at the highest point of the Mount of Olives, 830 metres above sea level, a small octagonal courtyard which you have to pay 5 NIS to enter. The Crusaders built a charming octagonal cloister to mark the spot where Jesus ascended into heaven 40 days after his resurrection. Walls and a roof were added by Armenian Christians in 1835, turning a charming open-air plaza into a small dark chapel. In the centre, in the bare rock, is a small hollow, traditionally the footprint of Jesus as he launched himself upwards and pushed the rock, which was trying to follow him, back to earth. It usually has no more than couple of people inside. The leaflet says,

"Visitors come here to cherish the last spot of Jesus on earth, read passages from texts and sermons, chant and light up candles."

The site is owned by the small mosque next door. The guide and caretaker, Mohammed, said that Christians were always welcome to pray there, and that lots came on Ascension Day. His son is a bus driver and works for an Israeli company - a fact which clearly brought him no joy.

Opposite the chapel/mosque is a small Greek Orthodox convent, which I had never visited before. Set in a large Orthodox cemetery, the nuns, all dressed in black, have a lovely small modern church with wonderful wall paintings. The entrance porch is a great evocation of the ascension, with the mystery of the Ascension of Jesus expressed by the open space of the doorway in the middle of the painting. I asked the sister in charge if I could look inside the church itself. She asked if I was

Orthodox. I said I was Anglican, and again asked if I could see the church. *"But you're not Orthodox!"* she exclaimed, and that was that.

At the corner is a large building with a very large Israeli flag. I remember the shock I felt in 1996 when I first saw it, and saw for myself the reality of the

creeping Israelification of East Jerusalem. The black water tanks on two of the buildings may be a sign that they are still lived in by Palestinians, and so their water supply is noticeably less reliable (and more expensive) than that of their Israeli neighbours.

Round the corner is one of my favourite places in Jerusalem, the Church of the Pater Noster. Since my last visit they have started charging 10 NIS, but it is still worth it. The first church on the site was built by Constantine's mother Helena about 330 and called the Church of the Apostles, or the Church of the Olive Grove. It was destroyed by the Persians in 614. A Crusader church was built in 1152 but destroyed after Salah-ed-Din's capture of Jerusalem in 1187. Princess Aurelia Bossi bought

the site in about 1860 and began searching for the cave where Jesus had tradiatinally taught his disciples. It has been French-owned ever since. She established a Carmelite convent and built the cloisters and church between 1868 and 1878. Between 1910 and 1915 an underground grotto and the Byzantine church were discovered and partly reconstructed. So the place is a tranquil mix of open-air buildings and gardens, with the walls of courtyard being covered with translations of the Lord's Prayer in

over 160 languages and dialects, such as Sardinian, Welsh and Cherokee. For me the centrepiece was the prayer in Aramaic and Hebrew, the actual languages of Jesus. The lush green gardens are a real oasis. I saw a small tabby cat being determinedly pursued by a three-legged ginger tom - I assume he won. At the side of the church is a beautiful olive grove with a fantastic view over Jerusalem. I was simply sitting and enjoying the peace when sadly I was told to leave. They close the site at lunchtime, 12.00 - 2.00. In Jerusalem you have to schedule your times of peace and quiet.

At the entrance to the church are two underground areas. One is the rediscovered Byzantine church. The other is the cave in which, according to the earliest tradition, Jesus taught his disciples about his second coming, as recorded in Mark 13. Indeed, in the 4th century the Tuesday of Holy Week was the big celebration in the church as they recalled the words of Jesus about the end of the age. Last Holy Week I went through the last seven chapters of Mark's gospel day-by-day, and discovered a whole new meaning to those strange and bewildering pronouncements, seeing them in the light of the coming crucifixion and resurrection.

From a scene of life to a scene of death, the enormous Jewish cemetery on the Mount of Olives. Jews have been buried here for over 2,500 years. There are 70,000 graves, including those of 13 Chief Rabbis. Devout Jews often wish to be buried there, facing the Temple Mount. It can cost as much as 200,000 NIS ($55,000) to reserve a grave, according to the Israel Business magazine Globes. Half way down are a collection of much more ancient graves, set in an enormous cave. The graves of the prophets Haggai, Zechariah and Malachi are supposed to be there. When I was here with Linda, an elderly Muslim appeared and showed us the caves,

but this time no one seemed to be around apart from a large German Shepherd dog. I moved on. The road down the Mount of Olives is narrow with walls on both sides. I missed out on Dominus Flevit church, (closed for lunch), where Jesus is supposed to have wept over Jerusalem on Palm Sunday. Dominus fleviti means "the Lord wept" It is a most attractive modern church, with an outstanding view of Jerusalem through the clear glass window at the east end. There are also loads of wonderful Byzantine floor mosaics dating from the 7th century.

I came to the bottom of the hill, hot, tired and thirsty. There, at last, was a small cafe but with apparently no one around and with little for sale. Eventually a middle-aged Palestinian appeared and I got a cup of tea. Then two young women came in, whom I had seen at various points on my walk down

the Mount of Olives. It turned out that they were a nun and her companion, wearing scarves and anoraks, and like me longing for a coffee. They were Slovakian and members of the Congregatio Jesu - Congregation of Jesus - a Roman Catholic order founded by an Englishwoman, Mary Ward (1585-1645), She wanted to found an active order for women, opening a school for girls in 1609 at St Omer, France. But in 1630 the Papacy ruled that her order should be disbanded because religious communities for women were only allowed to pray, not work. But she continued, founding schools for girls all over Europe. In 1639 she returned to England to establish free schools for the poor and nurse the sick, dying in the siege of York in 1645. In 2002 Pope John Paul II finally let the sisters have the same constitution as the Jesuits and the name that Mary Ward had wanted them to be called, Congregatio Jesu. The nuns were teachers at the Lutheran Schmidt School, near the Garden Tomb. The school has 520 Palestinian girls; 80% are Muslim; the rest come from various Christian churches, particularly Armenians. A classic example how Jerusalem is a melting pot of all faiths. Initially reluctant, they eventually agreed that I could take their photos.

A few yards away is the Garden of Gethsemane. This is a small enclosed square, filled with ancient olive trees, some of them 2,000 years old, probably the actual spot where Jesus waited for Judas on the last night of his life. It is a peaceful spot despite the 4-lane highway right next door. And it has benches where you can sit in the shade!

The church next door, the Church of All Nations, was built in 1924 by Roman Catholic Franciscans. It has wonderful mosaics inside and out, and reflects the night of prayer that Jesus spent, struggling to accept the Father's will. In the middle of the sanctuary is the rock on which Jesus might have prayed "If it is possible, let this cup pass me by. Nevertheless, not my will

but yours be done." The church has a seriousness about it and a recognition of the challenge of discipleship which many other churches do not show.

About a hundred yards away, in the valley bottom, lies the most extraordinary of all the churches in Jerusalem. Next to the busy 4-lane Jericho Road you will find wide stone steps leading down to a small plaza well below street level. In fact, if you go through a small door on the left you will find yourself at the rushing torrent of the underground river of Kidron. But

if you go ahead through a wide Crusader arch, you will find a further series of wide steps leading down to an Orthodox church celebrating the tomb of the Virgin Mary. (Other ancient tradition says she died in Ephesus. I guess that Jerusalem is the better bet - it is where her son James was bishop). The first church was built about 400 years later. Today's church is based on the

crypt of that church. It is full of icons and chandeliers and hangings and icons, all looking rather dusty, a bit like a neglected antique shop. But I am told that on major feast days, when there is celebration of the Orthodox liturgy at night, there are candles on both sides of the wide steps leading down, and it seems that you are walking down a river of light.

Back up in the winter sunshine, I climbed the road up to Lion Gate, also called St Stephen's Gate, one of the seven gates in the walls of the Old City. (The others are the Herod's gate, Damascus Gate, New Gate, Jaffa Gate, Zion Gate and Dung Gate). The last time I was here, the gate had been obscured by black netting as protection for the soldiers on guard there. I was pleased to see that that had been taken down, so you could see the historic arch properly. (There is also another gate, the Golden Gate, which leads directly into the Temple Mount. This has was closed off centuries ago, indeed blocked off by stone, and a Muslim cemetery established outside, to stop the Christian Messiah coming back that way).

Just a few yards inside St Stephen's gate you come to the complex surrounding

St Anne's Church. Again, you have to pay to go in, 8 NIS. St Anne's is a serene example of a Crusader church. Built in 1138, a Muslim theological school after Salah-ed-Din's victory in 1189, fallen into gross disrepair and finally given to France by the Ottomans in 1856 in gratitude for their part in the Crimean war. It is a lovely space with remarkable acoustics Everyone who enters has a try at singing and hearing themselves sound like some great Italian soprano or tenor. It is called St Anne's as it is supposed to be on the site of the home of Joachim and Anna, parents of the Virgin Mary, and the birthplace of Mary is meant to be in the basement, (which I think unlikely. Why move from the capital city to a one-horse village like Nazareth?)

St Anne's is also the most marvellous archaeological site. There are walls of buildings going back through crusader and Byzantine time to great cisterns built to provide water to Herod's

temple. This was the site of the Pool of Bethesda, the pool with five porticoes, where Jesus healed a paralysed man (John 5.1-8). No one knew what the five porticoes meant. Was it in the form of a pentagon? When the site was excavated by archaeologists, they found that the pool, destroyed in the Roman capture of Jerusalem in 68 AD, did have five porticoes, the fifth one acting as a bridge running midway between the two long sides. Surrounding the site are trees, a simple garden, an extraordinary number of kittens - and a French cafeteria. Another oasis!

But not enough of one. It was 3.00 and I still had not had anything to eat since 8.00. So to the Austrian Hospice, at the corner of the Via Dolorosa and Al-Wad Road. I walked up past  the Ecce Homo Convent (Behold the Man), passing a group of Chinese pilgrims on the way. I had stayed at Ecce Homo for a couple of nights in 1995, in a fairly spartan dormitory, being woken at 4.00 am by the very loud call to prayer from the tannoy in the neighbouring minaret. The convent houses the entrance to what is supposed to be the cell where Jesus was kept (unlikely) but also the enormous Roman cisterns, holding water for the city. I returned there in 2015, and the elderly nun who was taking the entrance money looked at me carefully and said, *"Don't I know you from somewhere?"* From a 3 day visit almost 20 years before!

At the corner of the road is a small area of large rounded stone slabs. This is the actual surface of the Roman street from 2,000 years ago. It was occupied by a squad of half a dozen Israeli soldiers and a police van. Apparently two weeks before, an Israeli soldier had been stabbed there by a Palestinian. The latter must have been pretty deranged to try that, but it is an index of the level of

tension which seems to me to get worse with each passing year. I told one of the solders about the paving slabs. He had had no idea, and was interested.

The Austrian Hospice is a real piece of Old Vienna. Once you have passed the security doors you are in an atmosphere of quiet sophistication. The cafe had a CD of some gentle Mozart being played. The Hospice had been built between 1855 and 1858 to the specifications of the Austrian emperor and became a pilgrim guest house. In 1918 the British turned it into an orphanage as well, but it was confiscated by the British at the start of the Second World War. In 1948 it became a military hospital and continued as a general hospital till 1967. It was finally restored to its original owners in 1985 and completely renovated in 1987. All the original wall and ceiling paintings were still there, underneath the plaster the Austrians had put on in 1948 for it to become a hospital.

I had an excellent goulash soup, a roll and a glass of beer. At the end of the corridor, by the chapel, is a large brass sculpture of the heavenly Jerusalem, built as a square with three gates in each side, and the river of the water of life flowing through the city (Revelation 21.12, 22.1) You can peer through the gates and over the top and see all the different activities that are going on. Quite magical.

Refreshed, I made my way to the Armenian Cathedral of St James, in the Armenian Quarter. (The Old City has four quarters, Christian, Muslim, Armenian and Jewish). You have to find your way through the warren of streets, up the Via Dolorosa, down Souk Khan al-Zeit, up David Street to the Jaffa Gate, and then it is a straightforward walk along Armenian Orthodox Patriarchate Road. The service started at 5.00, but I wanted to get there by 4.30 because I know that if I did not get there really early, I would have to stand throughout the service. I met Jo and Lesley just outside, but we had to stay in the courtyard till 4.45 when the doors were unlocked for Orthodox Vespers. We entered the darkness. There is no electric light, the only light is produced by candles in the chandeliers. There are no musical instruments, all music is by unaccompanied men's choir, providing a mesmeric sense of mystery. The reading of 1 Corinthians 1.18-31 was by a Syrian Orthodox priest: *"God's*

foolishness is wiser than human wisdom, and God's weakness is stronger than human strength." The gospel reading was Matthew 5.1-12: *"Blessed are you when people revile you and persecute you and utter all kinds of evil against you falsely on my account. Rejoice and be glad, for your* reward is great in heaven, for in the same way they persecuted the prophets who were before you."* The sermon was by an Armenian priest from America, where many Armenians fled after the Turkish-led genocide in 1915. He spoke about our present "All About Me" culture and how in contrast a hundred years ago the first thing that refugees from the Armenian genocide did was to build a church for the whole community and for future generations.

"We are called to be icons, images of our Creator...Just as Jesus became bread for us, we must become bread for each other and for the world."

At the end all the bishops, Orthodox and Catholic, gave the blessing.

Refreshments afterwards were in the main hall of the Seminary opposite, with plenty of room to move around and chat to people. I met John Howard, a Methodist minister who works at St Andrew's Scots Church. He came to Israel four years ago as an Ecumenical Accompanier in the EAPPI - Ecumenical Accompaniment Programme in Palestine and Israel, created in 2002 by the World Council of Churches. People come to act as a non-violent buffer between communities that are threatened and those communities doing the threatening.

John was called to help in the team at Yanoun. Yanoun (or Yanun) is a small Palestinian village in the north of the West Bank. Armed settlers had come into the village in 2002 and forced the villagers to leave. The villagers wanted to return but said they would only return if the EAPPI would guarantee to be present 24 hours a day 365 days a year. This is what happened, and the families returned to their village. EA's come from every nationality and each team only stays for three months because of the demanding and dangerous nature of the work, and because their visas last for three months and are very difficult to renew. John did his three month stint from February to April 2013, and the village is still there. But he felt a bit ambivalent, because protecting one village only puts its neighbour at risk. The village of Khirbet Tana, on the other side of the hill, has been destroyed by armed settlers six times.

The families now live in caves and the school is a tent. (In June 2017 the Israeli newspaper Haaretz reported on the situation with the headline: What happened at this Once-idyllic West Bank Spot Embodies the Israeli Occupation's Evils). John has a fantastic blog on therevdjohnhoward.wordpress.com, and the EAPPI has a blog on blog.eappi.org.

When I left the seminary compound, I heard one of my favourite pieces of music coming out of the speakers of the corner grocery shop, Missa Criolla, an Argentinian folk mass. I went in to speak to the Armenian shopkeeper and to congratulate him on his choice of music. We got into quite a conversation. He clearly believed in God, but was disgusted with the church. *"I'm secular, not religious,"* he insisted.
"Bishops and priests are called to tend the sheep. Nowadays when one sheep goes astray, they go after it and cut its throat."
I couldn't really think of anything to say, so went back to the hotel for supper.

Over supper Jo and Lesley talked about their trip to their former students in Nablus, and particularly about their visit to the church at Jacob's Well. The well is certainly the authentic site of the well that Jacob dug,and of Jesus' encounter with the woman of Samaria (John 4), because it is hard to move a narrow hole in the ground which is over 40 metres deep. In 1979 the priest there was butchered, almost certainly by a Zionist group who had threatened him a week before. In 2007 a new Greek Orthodox church was built there, but shortly before Jo and Lesley's visit someone broke in from the neighbouring refugee camp and some icons were stolen. This was a surprise because normally Palestinian Muslims respect churches. It was perhaps an indication of the dire economic situation Palestinians find themselves in because of the occupation.

TUESDAY 24th JANUARY

THE JOY OF GOD

I spent Monday in the Christian Quarter. Tuesday I planned to spend in the Moslem and Jewish Quarters. My first port of call was the al-Haram ash-Sharif or the Noble Sanctuary, otherwise called the Temple Mount. I had breakfast early and left the hotel at 8.00, because the hours you can enter the Temple Mount are quite restricted, normally from 7.30 to 11.00 and from 13.30 to 14.30. I had to leave time to walk through the city and get through the various security checkpoints, with my passport. Entrance to the Temple Mount is via a long an ugly wooden walkway from the far end of the plaza created

immediately after the 1967 Six Day War by demolishing 200 simple Arab houses. I did get a good view of the plaza at the Western Wall, and noted how many more women there were than men, and how much more space the men had than the women. Last time I noticed how lots of women wanted to take part, or at least hear, discussions about the Torah. They could do this by standing on white plastic chairs and leaning over the partition fence. Women are currently forbidden from reading a Torah scroll at the Western Wall.

Once inside the Noble Sanctuary, I met the unofficial guardian of the site, a handsome ginger cat, and settled down to enjoy the peace and space of the place. Its dimensions are the same as Herod's Temple; it is enormous, comprising one sixth of the area of the whole of the Old City. At its centre is the marvellous Dome of the Rock, constructed between 688 and 691. It has remained unchanged ever since, apart from tiles replacing the original

mosaics, and the re-gilding of the Dome, paid for by King Hussein of Jordan. It cost him $8.2 million and he had to sell one of his London houses to pay for it. In 1975 I was able to visit inside the Dome of the Rock, a symphony of light and

colour, and also the al-Aqsa Mosque (c. 710). It is enormous, holding 5,000 worshippers. I still remember the seemingly endless vista of coloured carpet that covered the floor. Now, however, only Muslims are allowed inside these amazing buildings. An Australian tourist in 1969 tried to set fire to al-Aqsa, believing it would hasten the second coming of Christ, but more significantly around 1983 two members of the Gush Emumim, Jewish extremists, plotted to blow up the Al Aqsa mosque and the Dome of the Rock. And since the second Intifada there have been occasional riots, for which Israel has

deployed up to 2,000 police and soldiers.

Security is obviously a reason why there are so many Israeli police and soldiers inside the Noble Sanctuary - a far cry from the 1970's, when the only Israeli presence was a soldier outside the

main entrance, ensuring that no Jews entered. Sadly, the security build-up does not stop anti-Muslim graffiti being daubed on the columns of the place. I met the Israeli graffiti-cleaning team, which now regularly comes to deal with graffiti.

I saw some Moslem women about to enter the Dome of the Rock and asked if I could go in. I was told firmly no, but a teenager offered to show me the inside. He took me round to the other side and showed me a microscopic hole in the thick wire mesh covering the windows, through which I could

see nothing. He then asked me for money. I gave him a 10 NIS coin, at which he exclaimed, *"This isn't money!"* I gave him a fairly curt response and moved on.

I went back through the Gate of the Cotton Merchants, built 1482, into the Souq al-

Qattanin, Market of the Cotton Merchants, a typical market street of the Old City. Unlike the open space of the Haram ash-Sharif, the Muslim Quarter is like a succession of semi-underground burrows. I followed the narrow Al-Wad street towards the Western Wall.

After a few yards was a Palestinian cafe, where I had a fruit juice, and made friends with a charming long-haired white cat who was insatiably curious about the contents of my travel bag. The Cafe itself looked quite ordinary on the outside, with plastic chairs and tables, but further in you saw that half of it was below street level and dated back hundreds of years.

While I was having my drink, an elderly, elegant man, Ba'asha, introduced himself to me. He showed me photos of the interior of the Dome of the Rock on his i-phone which were beautiful. He then started to tell me something of the inner history of the Noble Sanctuary. He told me of the prophet Mohammed's (Peace be upon him) night

journey. How an amazing winged horse took him from Mecca to Jerusalem, then up to the fourth heaven, then back to Mecca. When he told the people of Mecca about this, they ridiculed him, because he had not been absent, the journey must have taken no time at all. But he then amazed them by describing Jerusalem in detail, even though he had never visited it. In heaven he had met God, who told him to have Muslims pray 50 times a day. On the way back to earth he met Moses who asked him about his conversation with God.

Sabih Suleimi, a Crusader/
Mameluke drinking fountain

When Moses heard about the instruction to pray 50 times a day, he said, *"That's too many! Go back and ask God to allow Muslims to pray just 5 times a day."* Mohammed (p.b.u.h.) did so and God agreed. So Muslims have a lot to be grateful for to Jews. It is through Moses that they only have to pray 5 times a day!

Ba'asha's face shone with delight as he told me the story. I asked him if I could take his photo, but he said no. He had been a tourist guide for many years, but the Israeli authorities had brought in new regulations restricting the right to be a tourist guide only to people who had done their course. To do the course, you had to be fluent in Hebrew and English and have a degree. (That is how most Palestinian tourist guides, many of them Christian, lost their jobs).

It was only then that I realised had forgotten to bring any money with me. I left my bag in the care of the cat and went in search of a money-changer. I walked back along al-Wad Street in the direction of the Damascus Gate, where I knew I would find several. I found one quickly in a tiny shop-front. He was Armenian, called Garo, very cheerful, and spoke in a most peculiar voice. He had had throat cancer which had destroyed his vocal chords, and he now spoke through an artificial voice box. He had been born in Jerusalem in 1960, when it was still part of the kingdom of Jordan. The Old City and the West Bank were captured by Israel in the Six Day War in 1967. Eventually Garo moved to New York and lived there for 27 years. He then wanted to come back, so he had to apply for residency. It cost him $10,000 and he only had to wait 7 months! I asked him whether there was a problem with the Israeli authorities providing basic services for East Jerusalem. In reply, he focussed on the positives. Israelis were very good at fire-fighting, and were compassionate towards the sick. The hospitals were fine.

I returned to the cafe and paid my bill, then through the security barrier leading to the Western Wall and the Jewish Quarter. The security barrier was manned by another attractive cat, with the Israeli soldier acting a bit shame-faced about allowing his feline companion access to his radio transceiver.

On to the Western Wall. Up to 1967, there had been just a narrow passageway along the wall of Herod's Temple. Jews would come and pray there and insert scraps of paper with

prayers into the crevices between the great stone blocks. It was called the Wailing Wall, because of the centuries in which Jews all over the world would end the annual Passover celebration with the prayer/wish, *"Next year in Jerusalem!"* From 1948 to 1967 that had not been possible. After the capture of the Old City in the Six Days' War, General Dayan had handed over responsibility for the Temple Mount to Jerusalem's Muslim leaders, but the warren of streets in front of the Wailing Wall were demolished and a large open plaza was created in front of the newly-named Western Wall.

The explanatory leaflet is worth quoting.

"The only fragment of the Great Temple to survive the Roman destruction, the Divine Presence has never departed from the Western Wall… Its ancient stones stand testimony to a glorious Jewish past, a proud heritage and an extraordinary national rebirth… The Western Wall Plaza is the cleared area in front of part of the Western Wall. It allows a dignified approach to this holy place, and is a setting for national events: the Priests'

Blessing at Pesach (Passover) and Sukkot, candle-lighting on Chanukah, the swearing-in of Israel's police and armed forces recruits, and IDF and Jerusalem Day ceremonies."

I prayed at the Wall and found the Lord's Prayer particularly meaningful there. I sat and soaked up the atmosphere, watching men standing to pray, sitting to read devotionally, or just dozing. On reflection I think it is an entirely appropriate place to be the centre of Jewish worship and teaching, because there is nothing there except some ancient stones. It is what scandalised the ancient world, the fact that alone among the nations, Jews had no images. It is something that the Christian church could bear in mind, together with the emphasis that it is every Jew's responsibility to study his or her religion for themselves.

I walked up to the Jewish Quarter. My aim was to go on a tour of the Temple Institute, a museum with the political purpose of taking over the Temple Mount and rebuilding Herod's Temple on the site of the Dome of the Rock - an extreme  religious Zionist agenda. I had to wait for the 1.30 tour which

was in English, so I went for a wander through the Quarter. The Quarter had been heavily fought over in the 1948 war, all Jewish residents expelled from the Old City and the synagogues destroyed. Twenty years later, Jews returned and rebuilt. Everything looks brand spanking new, apart from archaeological sites. There is a passionate commitment to uncovering the past, for instance the foundations of the wall of Jerusalem during the first Temple period, pre-600 B.C.E., the Burnt House, destroyed by the Romans in 68 C.E., the synagogues destroyed or abandoned in 1948. All the residents are religiously orthodox, judging by the number of men and boys wearing their kippas - skull caps. But it also feels a bit lifeless after coming from the bustle of the souks in

the Muslim and Christian Quarters. One thing I noticed was how much of the rebuilding was supported by charitable gifts - and how all the gifts were heavily publicised, such as: FREE KITCHEN FOR THE NEEDY - sponsored by the Luxenberg family , New York.

I could not help being intrigued by a banner on a hostel advertising "Two nights free for all Birthright extensions". This refers to a programme offering all young Jews aged 18 - 26 from around the world a 10 day introduction to Israel, with free return flights. Since it started in 1999, over 500,000 young Jewish people from 64 countries have taken part. Having free air tickets to another continent is a great incentive. *"Your ten days are spent flying around the country on a bus full of sexually charged 20-somethings, waking up at sunrise and almost never sleeping or sleeping well, and running from one activity to the next. It's a really specific experience in which you are told what to do and when to do it; you have absolutely no say in what happens to you during those ten days."* (http://mishvoinmotion.com/extend-stay-birthright). A birthright extension is when people choose to postpone their return flight and spend longer in Israel in a more relaxed atmosphere. Various options can be: to take an academic Jewish learning programme, volunteer at an army base, learn Hebrew, go on a hike, or take the "Green Olives" tour which explores the Palestinian experience in Jerusalem, Bethlehem, Galilee and even the border of Gaza.

Needing a sit down and a coffee, I went to an open air cafe near the Temple Institute. On the table next to mine lay a black kippa without an apparent owner. The waiter asked if it was

mine. I replied, *"No, but we can be sure it belongs to a man."* He replied, *"It could be someone fooling us. It could be a girl who wants to be a man. Never assume!"*

I joined the 1.30 group at the Temple Institute. When I had been before, we had a live guide who could respond to questions. Now it was a pre-recorded tape. And no photographs were allowed. We were ushered through a series of rooms showing life-size models of everything needed for Temple worship: cups, shovels, flasks, censers, golden menorah, priestly garments and turbans, harps, lyres, rams' horn, silver trumpets, the showbread table and the ark of the covenant, together with paintings of the past and future Temple at work. (see the website templeinstitute.org, where the painting comes from).

The Institute's mission is to rebuild the Temple as it was in the days of Herod the Great. At my last visit the guide said that in one respect the restored Temple would be better than the original one - it would have underfloor heating! On the same occasion I asked the guide whether the demolition of the mosques and Dome of the Rock on the Temple Mount might not lead to massive war. She understood the question, but said that when the proper worship of God was restored to the Temple Mount, that would bring universal peace for everyone. I suppose that that is one posiible strategy.
The recorded talk, in American English, started:

"The sacred vessels you are going to be seeing on display here are not models, copies or replicas but actually kosher for use in the divine service of the Temple, made from the original materials, gold, silver and copper for example, according to the exact requirements of biblical law, the Torah and the sages of Israel...The Holy Temple is nothing less than the spiritual centre of all humanity and the focal point of man's direct unfolding relationship with God."

The end of the tour was a short film. Last time it had been a black-and-white film about the venerable rabbi, who seeing the flames of the capture of Jerusalem in the Six Day War had had a vision of a new era of peace through a restored Temple. It was moving. This time the film, in colour, showed the architect's vision for the new Temple complex, with a study centre, sanhedrin hall and modern conference facilities. It ended with a scene showing two children building a sand-temple on the seashore and the strap-line: *"The children will build."*   They had not apparently noticed what happens to sandcastles built on the edge of the sea.

Afterwards, in the Institute shop, I was intrigued by a photomap of Jerusalem, with the restored Temple superimposed on the Temple Mount. But that was not the only change. All the churches and mosques of Jerusalem, including the Church of the Holy Sepulchre had been airbrushed out. The shop assistant to whom I pointed this out had the grace to look embarrassed.

I walked up through Hurva Square to the Cardo,   or   Cardo Maximus.   This was the   main   street   in Roman and Byzantine times, leading directly north to the Damascus Gate.   Part has been preserved as a main street flanked by two roofed colonnades with shops either side. While there I overheard a conversation between an English visitor and a young Israeli. The Englishman asked if he knew how to get to Ramallah. The Israeli replied, *"I can't go anyway".* That is true. Since the Separation Wall was built, Palestinians can go into Israel only with difficulty and through checkpoints. Israelis are forbidden by the Israeli government to travel to the West Bank at all. The Palestinian city of Jericho used to have a flourishing casino which was a favourite venue for Jews from West Jerusalem. When the government made trips like this illegal for Israelis, the casino had to close.

However, I told the young man that if he stuck with me I could get him the information on getting to Ramallah, whether by bus, taxi or "sheroot" - shared taxi. Jo and Lesley would know exactly how to get there. *"Whatever happens, you must make sure to take your passport or you might not get out again".*

The young man was Andrew Markham, a teacher in a private school in Turkey. He was happy to come with me on my planned itinerary to St Mark's Syrian Orthodox church, to the service at the Lutheran church and finally to supper in the Knights' Palace Hotel.

St Mark's is an ancient church hidden away in the back streets of the Christian Quarter.The church has elaborate decoration in the Orthodox tradition, and a famous icon of the Virgin and child which we were not allowed to photograph. But

downstairs is a simple bare room made of massive stone blocks, which the Syrian Orthodox believe was the actual site of the Last Supper. I think it is well possible. It is a pretty good guess that the Last Supper was held in the house of the mother of St Mark, which continued to be a major meeting place for early Christians from then on. When Peter was imprisoned, it was at that house that his friends gathered to pray for him (Acts 12). All that was in it was a simple altar, a rug and a few white plastic chairs. Andrew and I sat in silence there for a long time, breathing in the spiritual atmosphere of the place.

Upstairs, on the ground level, was the church proper. A convent sister was on duty, Sister Justina. She was quite a fierce lady, especially guarding the Icon of the Virgin Mary from any camera-toting tourists. It is, after all, the oldest painting of the Virgin, having been painted on leather from life by St Luke. To me it looked rather more like an 18th Century painting, but who am I to say?

Sister Justina's brother Yusuf is a Syrian Orthodox priest in England. With joy, she told me of a remarkable spiritual experience she had had in St Mark's church. They had had a wonderful service for Pentecost (commemorating the event of the Holy Spirit sweeping over the original disciples two months after Jesus' resurrection). Afterwards a Tel Aviv policeman had come into the church, who only spoke Russian and Hebrew. Sister Justina knew only Syrian and English. And yet the two of them conversed with perfect understanding for an hour, without realising something strange was going on. Three months later he came back, and they did not understand one other at all. He got very angry, thinking that she was making a fool of him. Fortunately her sister and her husband had arrived in the nick of time - for some reason they had taken the car instead of walking as they usually did. They were able to assure the angry policeman that Sister Justina did indeed not know Hebrew. She realised that their earlier conversation, in the aftermath of the Pentecost celebrations had simply been a wonderful gift of God.

Andrew and I made our way back through the Christian Quarter to the Church of the Redeemer for the 5 o'clock service. It was a good Lutheran service, with hymns and excellent music, such as two solos by Hildegard of Bingen and Heinrich Schütz. Much of the service was in English, Arabic and German, but the intercessions were in English, German, Arabic, Finnish, Dutch, Danish and Swedish with an Arabic response: *"Ya-ah Rab ah-salami amter alayna salam" - God of peace, rain down peace on us".* The main reading was the long story in Acts 9 of the conversion of Saul from a persecutor of the church to an ardent evangelist; how Christ confronted him outside Damascus, and he became instantly blind. After three days a local disciple of Jesus, Ananias, prayed for him, "something like scales fell from his eyes" and he was healed.. It was followed by a gospel reading - the Beatitudes from Matthew 5. The Lutheran bishop of Jerusalem and the Holy Land, Dr Munib Younan, based in Amman, gave the sermon.

"The story of Saul's conversion reveals something important about our call to Christian unity. Like Saul, we have heard the voice of Jesus. Like Saul, we want to follow. We want to serve him. We want to be one, as the Father and the Son are one! But in spite of our prayers, unity has not come immediately. In spite of our willingness, we are still on a journey, of which we cannot see the ending.

We must admit that as churches, we are like Saul. Our desire to follow is not enough. Our desire for Christian unity is not enough. Like Saul, we are first in need of healing.

As churches, we have scales on our eyes which keep us from seeing Christ in the other, even other Christians. These scales are called tradition, theology, history, pride, status quo, and sometimes deep pain from past disagreements. Like Saul, we cannot follow the Lord's call until these scales have fallen from our eyes. We cannot be one, until we can see the image of Christ in each other clearly.

The year 2017 marks the 500th anniversary of the Reformation. For Lutherans, this is a moment of joy and repentance. We celebrate the reformers who gave us great works of systematic theology on justification by faith. We celebrate that the Bible has been translated into the vernacular. We celebrate the music and art that has come from the Reformation movement.

But we do not celebrate the division of the church. Our Lord has not called us to congratulate ourselves on 500 years of living, praying, and serving separately from our sisters and brothers. Both Lutherans and Catholics have heard the call of Christ to seek reconciliation. For this reason, fifty years ago, the Lutheran and Catholic churches began a dialogue...

One outcome of this fifty-year journey of dialogue was last year's worship service of Common Prayer in Sweden, co-hosted by Pope Francis, by Rev. Martin Junge, the General Secretary of the Lutheran World Federation, and by myself as the President of the LWF. This Common Prayer, which took place on Reformation Day at the beginning of this 500th anniversary year, was an historic reconciliation. It was a moment that no one could have envisioned fifty years ago. I was deeply honoured to have co-hosted and co-led, with the

Pope, such a visible sign of Christian unity, and to sign a joint statement of ongoing reconciliation…

One thing we can be sure of, and that is that when we are seeking God's will, God hears our prayers. Our prayers for unity have already been answered through the trust and friendship we share across our various traditions. Trust and friendship make it easier to be in partnership—and make it much harder to be in competition.

I would like to close with a prayer, written by an Anglican clergyman, and which is found in nearly every Lutheran hymnal. Let us pray:

> *"Lord God, You have called your servants to ventures of which we cannot see the ending, by paths as yet untrodden, through perils unknown. Give us faith to go out in good courage, not knowing where we go but only that Your hand is leading us and Your love supporting us; through Jesus Christ our Lord. Amen."*

Afterwards a great crush of uniting Christians jostled together in the church's refectory next door, sampling plastic glasses of squash and biscuits. Andrew got chatting to Carrie, the

Lutheran pastor. To their mutual amazement they discovered that both knew each others' families! A real Jerusalem moment. I met Sebi Behrens, a German photographer, who was about to have an exhibition on Jerusalem churches. His photos were beautiful and poetic and sometimes slyly humorous. You can see some of them on www.sebibehrensphoto.com.

Andrew came back with us for supper, together with Sister Patricia from the Tantur Ecumenical Institute. Tantur is housed in a large stone building which overlooks Bethlehem to the south and Jerusalem to the north. Started in 1972, it is an ecumenical oasis of learning,  dialogue, prayer and community amid the political and religous complexity of Israel and the Palestinian Territories. Its mission is to work towards Christian unity, to contribute to dialogue between people of the Abrahamic faiths, (Jews, Christians and Muslims), and to peace building, particularly between Israelis and Palestinians. It is linked to the Universty of Notre Dame who use it as a focus for theology and peace studies. Their website is www.tantur.org

WEDNESDAY 25th JANUARY

LIGHT AND DARKNESS

After breakfast I walked down Casa Nova and Greek Patriarchate Road towards Jaffa Gate. I wrote some postcards in a cafe on the corner. Just a few steps away is a small post office where I could post them. Opposite is the police station of the Old City. I had to go there in 2014 after a postcard seller on the Mount of Olives had dipped into my bag and stolen my mobile phone. The policeman who took the details had said wryly, *"Welcome to Jerusalem."*

I walked up along the outside walls to the bus stop on Jaffa Road (or Yafo Road). It is almost opposite the Bible Society in Israel shop. I did not go into it because of a disturbing experience I had two years before. I had gone into the shop and started a long discussion with the manager, who was convinced that the establishment of the state of Israel was a fulfilment of biblical prophecy, and that Jews had the right to occupy the whole of former Palestine. I had said that I did not think that God used unclean methods.
"Such as?" he demanded.
"Well," I replied, *"Menachem Begin was head of the Irgun, a terrorist group, and was responsible for the massacre of Deir Yassin in 1948; he became Prime Minister. Yitzhak Shamir, head of the Stern Gang, was responsible in 1948 for the assassination of Count Bernadotte, the United Nations envoy* (who almost brought about an agreement to make Jerusalem in international city); *he became Prime Minister. And Ariel Sharon, the general-in-command in the Lebanese war; he was responsible for the massacre of Palestinians in the Sabra and Shatila refugee camps and an Israeli commission,* (the Kahane commission), *said he was unfit to hold political office; he became Prime Minister."*
The manager got more and more angry and at last burst out furiously, *"That proves that you are covered with an evil spirit!"*

So I walked along Jaffa Road looking for a bus stop for bus 66.

I found one, but it did not mention 66 - at least not in English lettering. I asked a young Israeli mother if 66 went from there, because it was not on the bus sign. She said, yes.
I said, *"Jerusalem is a very confusing place."*
She replied, *"We have to love Jerusalem."*

My destination was the Israel Museum, a fascinating place where you could easily spend several days. I had half a day, so was not able to visit the neighbouring Bible Lands Museum, with its archaeological displays of the history of Israel and the Ancient Near East done so as to be appreciated by people

of all faiths.   Perhaps next time. On the other side of the valley is the Knesset or Parliament, where 120 representatives debate and form a variety of unstable alliances. The present make-up of the Knesset (in July 2017) is as follows:

     Likud (right-wing) - 30;
     Zionist Camp (centre-left) - 24;
     Joint List (four Arab parties) - 13;
     Yesh Atid (centrist) - 11;
     Kulanu (centrist) - 10;
     Beit Yehudi (Jewish Home, Orthodox Jewish,
         religious Zionist) - 8;
     Shas (ultra-Orthodox religious) - 7;
     United Torah Judaism (ultra-Orthodox) - 6;
     Meretz (secular, two-state solution) - 5;
     Yisrael Beitenu (Israel Our Home, mainly Russian

Jews, secularist, right-wing) - 5;
Independent - 1.
The government is currently a coalition between Likud, Kulanu, Beit Yehudi, Shas, and United Torah Judaism. So the government survives thanks to the 21 votes of the ultra-Orthodox religious parties.

On entering the Museum I saw the smallest Bible in the world - not I guess including the New Testament. It is the Nano Bible, the size of a grain of sugar, and on that tiny silicon chip all 1.2 million letters have been inscribed You need a microscope with a 10,000 magnification factor. In 2009 the former President of Israel, Shimon Peres, presented it to Pope Benedict XVI. I do not know if the Pope was also given a microscope to go with it

My first priority was to see the model of 1st century Jerusalem, or the Second Temple Model as the museum calls it. I had first seen this in 1963, when it was in the grounds of the Holy Land Hotel. At that time there was a military border separating the Old City from West Jerusalem. In 2006 it was moved to its present site in the Israel Museum, and I visit it each time I come to Jerusalem. It was (and is) amazing to see such a large and detailed model of the Jerusalem which Jesus knew, the Pool of Bethesda, where the paralysed man was healed, the Temple with the enormous Court of the Gentiles which Jesus cleared the traders out of, the High Priest's house, the Antonia fortress from which the Romans kept control of the city, the palaces of Pontius Pilate and Herod Agrippa, and the small rocky outcrop where he hung on the cross for six hours. It was so fascinating that I used an entire roll of film for slides.

The Temple built by Herod the Great. Within the enormous court of the Gentiles is the Court of Israel, then the Court of the Priest, then the Holy Place, finally the Holy of Holies.

The Pool of Bethesda with the Antonia Fortress and the Temple in the background.

Lower Jerusalem. My guess is that was in this warren of streets that Jesus had his Last Supper with his disciples.

The rock of Golgotha, outside the city wall.

Next door is the most significant exhibition in the Museum, the Dome of the Book. Here are displayed the Dead Sea scrolls, the writings of the Essene community at Qumran before the revolt of 66 C.E., These include the most ancient Biblical texts discovered, which pushed back the earliest known Hebrew copies of the Old Testament books by a thousand years. They also describe how the Essene community functioned, which I found very interesting indeed. In the dark tunnel leading to the exhibited scrolls are lighted panels quoting from the Essene writings. I had long assumed that the early followers of Jesus had close links with the Essenes, simply because they are the only contemporary Jewish group to have no mention at all in the New Testament. Here are some of the explanations with actual quotations in italics.

"Essenes aimed to establish, in the desert, a community that would serve as a 'spiritual temple', or, as the scrolls put it, "a temple of man", that is, a human substitute for the Temple in Jerusalem. Their communal meals may have even symbolised the sacrificial rites... Their 'Songs of Sabbath Sacrifice" were considered a substitute for the sacrifices that were offered on the Sabbath in the Temple."

"Prayer rightly offered shall be as an acceptable fragrance of righteousness, and perfection of way as a delectable free will offering. (Community Rule IX.5)

"When he has completed one year within the Community ... his property and earnings shall be handed over to the Bursar of the Congregation." (Community Rule VI.18-19)

Josephus writing in the first century C.E commented about the community meals:
"They then go into the refectory in a state of ritual cleanliness as if it were a holy temple and sit down in silence.... The priest says the grace before meat: to taste food before this prayer is forbidden. After breakfast he offers a second prayer; for at the beginning and the end they give thanks to God as the Giver of life."

"And when they become members of the community in Israel according to these rules, they shall separate from the habitations of unjust men and shall go into the wilderness to prepare there the way of Him." (Community Rule VIII.13)

The Dome of the Book is roofed by a magnified representation of one of the pottery tops that protected the scrolls. White symbolises the sons of light and the constantly flowing water represents the purity rituals which were so important for the community, as indeed they are for religiously orthodox Jews today, as well as keeping the temperature and humidity inside constant. But the Dome of the Book is balanced, as the Essene theology was balanced, by the black basalt wall which you can see behind. This represent the sons of darkness, whose fate is to be consigned to the wrath of God and the dustbin of history. I wonder whom these two monuments represent today.

Then on to the magnificent archaeology gallery.

During the Chalcolithic or Bronze Age, c.3300 - 1200 B.C.E., there was a long period of stability and peace. This is seen by the immense number of bronze implements that were found at the sanctuary on the cliffs of Ein Gedi, overlooking the Dead Sea. In 1976 I visited it by accident, going for a wander after enjoying the waterfall below. But this whole civilisation suddenly disappeared, perhaps because of a catastrophic war?

There are some wonderful Canaanite remains - mortuary jars, statues of a king and a Canaanite shrine.

Canaanite mortuary jars

A Canaanite king

A Canaanite shrine

An Israelite temple from Arad

1996 I had visited Arad in southern Israel. The Canaanite city had been completely destroyed, but Israelites had built a replacement city nearby in the tenth century B.C.E.
It had been wonderfully preserved,but the most remarkable feature was that it contained a temple, built on the same lines as Solomon's Temple in Jerusalem.

For instance, it had two pillars standing between the area of sacrifice and the Holy of Holies. In Jerusalem the two pillars were made of bronze and had names, Boaz and Jachin, (see 1 Kings 7.13-22). Now the Arad temple, or I rather hope a copy of it, stands in the Israel Museum.

I then went to the Jewish art and life gallery, showing how Jews have maintained their cultural and religious life in all corners of the Diaspora - the whole world where Jews have been scattered over the centuries. I really liked the synagogues gallery, where various old synagogues had been

recreated. I was struck by the elegance of the synagogue in Venice, the colourful folk art paintings in the synagogue in South Germany - saved because it got used as a barn, and particularly by the 16th century one in Cochin, India.

I had visited this when I spent two months in south India in 1983. I was told that Jews first settled there when fleeing from the destruction of Jerusalem by Nebuchadnezzar. King of Babylon, in 587 B.C.E. They had brought with them two silver trumpets used in worship. Unfortunately, these no longer survive, because two members of the community had had a quarrel and they broke the trumpets on each others' heads!

I moved on to the art gallery - a superb display of modern art. The early 20th century section was very interesting. One large triptych titled "Firstfruits" expressed the original vision of Zionism, which was to create a new type of Jew through working the land, a Jew who was physically strong, and secular. It was by one of the most important Jewish artists of the time, Reuven Rubin, a Romanian Jew, who arrived in Palestine in 1923 at the age of 30, and who saw *"sunshine, the sea, the halutzim (pioneers) with their bronzed faces and open shirts, the Yemenite girls, and children with enormous eyes. A new country, a new life was springing up around me."*
                                        (Rubin, My Life and Art)

The central panel shows a pioneer couple offering a melon and bananas as first fruits. Next to them is a traditional Yemenite Jewish couple, quite passive, offering their son. The side panels show Palestinians who are sleeping or playing a flute, letting life pass them by.

Another painting shows the joy that the early settlers felt in the land.

But there is a caveat in my mind. In 1932 the leader of the Kameraden, the Jewish youth group which my father belonged to, decided to emigrate to Palestine. One of my father's friends, Fritz Levinger, started a protest petition condemning him for taking land away from Palestinian farmers. The following year Hitler came to power and Fritz, later Perez, Levinger himself emigrated to Palestine.

The past, present and future of the relationship between Israel and Palestine is starkly presented in a work by a Palestinian visual artist, Sharif Waked, living in Nazareth. Titled "Jericho First" it starts with an image from an eighth century mosaic floor at Hisham's Palace in Jericho of a lion attacking a gazelle and gradually proceeds in a series of images in which the gazelle is completely swallowed up except for one hoof.

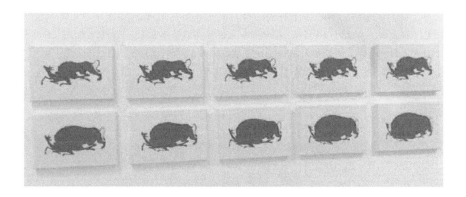

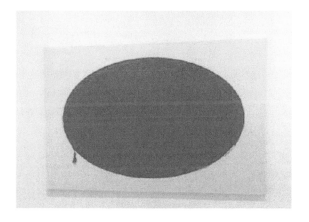

"Although it refers to the local conflict between Israel and the Palestinians, the work reaches out beyond this context to depict an unending universal struggle between weak and strong, innocent and cruel, good and evil."

From there I went to the top floor to a photographic exhibition on Modern Architecture in British Mandate Palestine. In particular it showed how migrants from  Germany brought with them the new Bauhaus style of architecture, with bold clean lines, and a sensitivity to the interrelationship possible between inside and external spaces. It is because of so many high quality modern houses in Tel Aviv that it has been declared a World Heritage site.

Why, then, I ask myself, are the modern Jewish settlements monuments to ugliness and the destruction of landscape?

On the same level was an remarkable exhibition, "Behold the Man: Jesus in Israeli Art". There were photos and pictures  which referenced famous Christian paintings, such a Palestinian mother and child; it is imbued with enormous sadness, much like paintings of the Virgin Mary with the dead body of Christ in her lap, an amalgamation of a Nativity and a Pietá. What future can she hope for her son?

There was an extraordinary photo by Nes Adi of a group of young Israeli soldiers, none of them wearing a kippa, called: "Untitled (Last Supper). The squad are all chatting or bickering between themselves. The leader is isolated, looking ahead to an uncertain future.

"Bedouin Crucifixion" is a sculpture by an Israeli artist Igael Tumarkin, created out of an assemblage of found objects in Bedouin camps. He has made a series of artworks drawing attention to the plight of the Bedouins in Israel.

The most extraordinary painting of all is Costel's Crucifixion. Moshe Costel was born in Palestine before the British Mandate to a Jewish religious family. Tragically, his newborn baby and his wife both died in childbirth. He secluded himself in a

monastery to deal with his grief, and while there painted this crucifixion.

The inscription on the cross, in Hebrew, reads "Costel the Jew". Earlier versions had had the inscription "Yeshu'a", the Hebrew name of Jesus. (Not "Yeshu" which is how Jews often referred to him, which means, "May his name be obliterated").

Costel told nobody about this painting, and it was only discovered in a locked cupboard after his death in 1992.

I then made my way back the main entrance. Sadly I did not have enough time to take in the great sculptures they have in the art garden. However, I did pass this genial sculpture placed, rather incongruously, at the entrance of the Youth Wing for Art Education.

I got one of West Jerusalem's yellow taxis. My aim was the Franciscan church in the Latin Patriarchate, and he said he would drop me inside Jaffa Gate - whether because of security fears I don't know.

Like most Israelis, he was a man of few words and a combative style. I said that I thought that there were three types of Israelis - secular, religious and settlers. He responded, *"Only three?!"* I asked about the previous mayor of Jerusalem, Teddy Kollek, who had tried to develop Jerusalem as a city for all its communities, Jewish, Muslim and Christian. My driver said, *"He was good, very good."*

Teddy Kollek was born in Vienna in 1911. In 1965 he became mayor of West Jerusalem and remained mayor of the united city until 1993, winning five elections. he said,
"I got into this by accident [...] I was bored. When the city was united, I saw this as an historic occasion. To take care of it and show better care than anyone else ever has is a full life purpose. I think Jerusalem is the one essential element in Jewish history. A body can live without an arm or a leg, not without the heart. This is the heart and soul of it."

His first act after the capture of East Jerusalem in 1967 was to send in milk for the Arab children. He strongly advocated religious tolerance. He has been called "The greatest builder of Jerusalem since Herod". In his first year as mayor he founded the Israel Museum. At its 25th anniversary in 1990 he was given the title of "father of the museum".

The present mayor Nir Barkat, mayor since 2008, is a successful and wealthy businessman, who has attracted numerous hi-tech firms in. He takes no salary. He is Likud and has no time for women's groups who oppose the creeping segregation, e.g.on buses, which religious Jews try to enforce. In October 2015 he said that all Israelis should carry a gun as "a duty".

Once inside Jaffa gate, I walked up Greek Patriarchate Road and Casa Nova to our hotel, and from there a short way down Franciscan Road and through a series of courtyards to the Church of St Saviour Jerusalem, Ecclesia Sanctissimi Salvatoris Hierosolymis, rebuilt 1885. The church belongs to the Franciscans, who have been the Catholic Church's official guardians of the Holy Land sites since St Francis founded it in 1216. The first thing that  struck me was the most marvellous Nativity scene, almost life-size. Appropriate, because it was St Francis who in 1223 created the first Christmas crib with local people taking part.

The church itself was just as splendid. I sat near the front and found myself entirely surrounded by nuns. There was Sister Marie-Hélène of Ecce Home, Sisters of the Rosary, who asked, *"Please pray for us,"* and Benedictine sisters for the convent at Abu Ghosh. This is a Palestinian village about 7 miles outside Jerusalem, with a magnificent Crusader church with most of its wall-paintings intact. On Sunday they sing the most beautiful setting of the Mass. I have been to the Sunday service with them three times, and used to have a cassette tape of their singing. (Yes, it was that long ago!).

The service started with the choir singing a hymn. The readings were in Italian, English and Arabic. Genesis 19.15-26 told the story of Lot's escape form Sodom before it was destroyed by fire from heaven. In Philippians 3.7-14 Paul said, *"I even consider everything as a loss because of the supreme good of knowing Christ Jesus my Lord."* The Gospel was Luke 9.57-62, in which Jesus says, *"No one who sets his hand to the plough and looks to what was left behind is fit for the kingdom of God."*

Brother Nerwan Banna, the local parish priest gave the sermon

in Arabic; it was clearly a call to greater determination to bring about Christian unity. This is what Cardinal Pizzabella, the Apostolic Administrator has said:

"Every year, the atmosphere is more positive, there is more and more opportunity to build something new. Nothing sensational, there will not be huge changes, but there has been a rise in the awareness of belonging to a single body which is the Church of Christ. Then the results are obvious: restorations in the tomb (i.e. the Church of the Holy Sepulchre), or changes in the parishes, more and more obvious unity activities, that during this week represent a milestone that reveals the journey of all these years."

The Intercessory prayers were in Italian, English, French, German, Spanish and Hebrew, with a response in Arabic: *"Istajeb ya Rab'*, meaning *"Grant, O Lord".*

After singing "Make me a channel of your peace", first verse in Italian, the second verse in English, we were welcomed *"in the custodia Curia to share a moment of brotherhood."*

the refectory there was squash and nibbles, which I helped hand round. I got into a good conversation with three Jerusalemites: Ken, an American carpenter with a long wispy white beard, who had lived here for 23 years; Nino a Greek dentist who lived and worked a few yards from our hotel; he had an enthusiastic opinion about everything and a somewhat overpowering sense of humour; and Mike who I do not remember so well. I mentioned the exhibition of modern architecture in Tel Aviv and asked why modern Israel seemed so keen to make Israel uglier with all their new buildings. They replied that it was a global problem. All over the world high rise buildings are springing up, in Tel Aviv, in London etc. Money and pride conspire to put up dreadful modern buildings everywhere. When Teddy Kollek was mayor of Jerusalem, he tried to limit new buildings to three stories, in keeping with the rest of the city. But when Menachem Begin became Prime Minister, everything changed. He was the most Ashkenazi (or West European) politician of them all. But he based his party on support from the Sephardic Jews, (Jews from North Africa and the Middle East). They tended to have large families so there were lots of young sephardim, lots of homes were needed, and the development of high-rise apartments became inevitable. As the singer/songwriter

Carly Simon said, *"They found paradise, and put up a parking lot."*

(This class distinction between Ashkenazi and Sephardic Jews is not often mentioned. I remember being told in 1963 that if you wanted to be part of the upper classes of Israel, you would go to classical concerts in Tel Aviv and speak Hebrew with a German accent. If you were a Sephardic Jew the best you could hope for was to be a bank manager in Beersheba).

At supper Jo and I were on our own. Lesley had gone with Sister Patricia to a concert by the Jerusalem Symphony Orchestra to hear Mozart's Violin Concerto in D, Bartok's Concerto for Orchestra and a new piece by Moshe Zorman called "City Pictures". Sister Patricia was a good friend of the percussionist.

During the day, Lesley and Jo had visited Hebron and a Bedouin village in the Negev. Jo was quite shaken. by it all.

"We went to a weaving project in a village 18 km from Beer-Sheva. It was a project set up for Bedouin women. They usually set up their looms outside and they make lovely stuff, and they bring it to the centre to assemble it for orders. They make everything to order so you can have any colours you like, not just the traditional blues and reds. We noticed three of the women setting up a vat in the dyeing shed. At first I thought they were preparing to dye the yarn but no, they were making a huge vat of the traditional lentil soup.

I had seen on Facebook about a Bedouin village being demolished not far away, so we drove there There had been violent clashes. The information had come originally from the Israeli Committee Against House Demolitions, though this is just one of a number of organisations who do this campaigning.

"The village, Umm al-Hiran, took some finding, we drove up and down and out into the wilderness. I was really surprised when we found it, because it's in the middle of nowhere. The

clashes are about Israel wanting the land to build a village, but there is no reason why they need to build right there when all around is nothing! Why do people have to be moved from their homes to make space for a new Israeli village? I mean, they've got the whole of the Negev to choose from!

"Anyway, so far ten houses have been demolished and two people killed. There's about 20 simple houses left, and they all will go. It was absolutely pitiful. When I first saw one of the houses I could hardly believe it, it was such a small pile of rubble. But when you think that ten people might have been living in each of those houses. .. and the animal shelters, also all destroyed. Now they are just piles of twisted metal, breeze blocks etc.

"The men were in a separate marquee receiving condolences. Normally they would do this over three day and you sit for an hour and have a sip of unsweetened coffee. As foreigners we were welcomed in to sit with the men. They told about the day this happened. There were soldiers and police and helicopters and bulldozers, the whole panoply of a war. People were shot on both sides, police were injured by other police, it was mayhem apparently. One of the police was killed. An Israeli Arab MK (Member of the Knesset) had been injured. What was really heart-breaking was the bafflement of the heads of families. They could not understand why Israel was doing this to them. The Bedouins had no quarrel with Israel, and Israel had given them the land sixty years ago. They'd not just set up their tents, they'd built houses (even though they are very simple with no municipal services – an 'unrecognised' village.)

"Lesley and I were shown round by two young men, one a medical student in Moldavia, the other the son of the teacher who was shot, also studying medicine but in the Ukraine. The villagers said that, even though he is the eldest son, it is far more important for him to go back and get qualified and then return.
"The women and children were living in a huge marquee, and we saw the carpet project vehicle come bumping over the

rough road to deliver the soup. The young men were salvaging bits of anything they could to make make-shift tents and pens for their animals. Traditionally they would take them over the neighbouring hills and fields and, you know, roam and graze the land, but that lifestyle is disrupted now.

"One lady came out of a demolished house with just a bag and put the bag down on the ground. She had salvaged a plastic hand mirror and a few bits and pieces from the kitchen. Just awful. "

Note 1. The website of the Israeli Committee Against House Demolitions is icahd.org

Note 2. I spoke to my Friend Mary-Clare in Tel Aviv on Friday about this. She had heard a different story. Later she emailed me with the following statement from a friend:

"A joint Israeli-Arab independent team were there to investigate. Their finding were quite horrifying. Most of the tenants in that illegal village were willingly resettled in a modern recognised village receiving generous compensations by the Israeli government.
However about 10% were coerced to stay, incited by "human rights" activists from Israel and abroad, joined by the PA authorities, all of whom paid them generous amounts of money, so that they would not budge from their evacuated village.
I spoke to my shocked Bedouin friend a few days after he returned from the investigation, he said that he could not understand why was this done to his tribe and why they allowed themselves to be exploited this way. Nonetheless, I think that the Israeli police acted brutally and despicably and this was widely criticised in the Israeli media by the way."

Like everything in Israel/Palestine, there are always at least two narratives. But how can a village be "illegal" after 60 years?

THURSDAY 26th JANUARY

FACING GIANTS

Had a slow start this morning as my first call was to go to the Swedish Christian Centre at 10.30. I had met the director, Anne-Sophie, at the refreshments after the service on Monday evening at the Armenian Orthodox Seminary. Jo and Lesley had recommended it to me because it is a really comfortable place and has a superb rooftop view of the Old City. To find it you have to go to the square inside Jaffa Gate and stand in front of the Tower of David. From there, you have a

remarkable 360° view starting at the Tower of David - nothing to do with David (a Byzantine error), but the bottom stone courses are from a palace of Herod the Great, with Crusader and Ottoman additions. There is an interesting historical and archaeological museum inside, if from a rather one one-sided point of view. Turning anti-clockwise you have the police station, the Armenian Patriarchate Road, down which Orthodox Jews drive to get to the Jewish Quarter, the post office, Christ Church and its cafe, the Christian Information Centre, and at the side of an alley, a small door leading to the Swedish Christian Centre.

Anne-Sophie welcomed me into the delightful centre, in an old Ottoman-era building, a great place for a relaxing cup of coffee, even if you are not Swedish. She had been delayed because of a meeting with the senior pastor of the Lutheran Church of the Redeemer. The Centre is very ecumenical, welcoming Methodists, Baptists, everyone really apart from members of the Swedish Lutheran church, who have their own theological centre in West Jerusalem. How Jerusalem!

She took me up to the roof, where there are great views of the Old City,including the domes of the Church of the Holy Sepulchre, two domes and the bell-tower, the minaret of the adjoining mosque and the tower of the Church of the Redeemer, with the tower of the Hebrew University on Mount Scopus in the distance and, further round, the Temple Mount and the Mount of Olives.

I got a taxi from Jaffa Gate and met Jo and Lesley at the door of the offices of Sabeel in West Jerusalem We had come for the weekly communion service and fellowship lunch which happens every Thursday. Sabeel, which is Arabic for "the way" or a "channel/spring of water", is an Ecumenical Christian Liberation Theology Centre, founded by the former Dean of St George's Cathedral, Naim Ateek, a

greatly respected figure in the Jerusalem churches. Sabeel *"strives to develop a spirituality based on love, justice, peace, nonviolence, liberation and reconciliation for the different national and faith communities."* In particular, the group aims to *"promote a more accurate international awareness regarding the identity, presence and witness of Palestinian Christians as well as their contemporary concerns..."* Its work involves:

> Exploring the meaning of the Gospel
> in the Palestinian situation.
> Supporting the Palestinian Christian community.
> Working for a more accurate international awareness
> of the suffering of the Palestinian people.

There were only seven of us sitting round a candle for the service. These were Jo, Lesley and me; Omar Haramy who led the service; Sausan Bitar, a Palestinian helper; Tina, a Canadian who has lived in Jerusalem for 10 years and who works with an American tour company; and Erdmuthe from Frankfurt; she had come out as an Ecumenical Accompanier and was shortly returning to Germany.

Remarkably, the Bible reading was the Beatitudes from Matthew 5 - again! I was asked to read it, which I did slowly, and then we had 5 minutes silence to reflect on it, followed by a general discussion before moving on to the communion itself. I felt very privileged to be part of this little group, because each of them had embodied in their own lives what it meant to mourn, to be at the bottom of the heap, to hunger and thirst for righteousness, to practice mercy, to act as peacemakers, to be attacked by those who resented their stand for the oppressed. Here are a few of the points that were made during the gentle discussion following the reading.

Omar:
At the Sabeel conference in Oxford, someone said that the Beatitudes are not about politics, they are about character.
Jo:
The Beatitudes are about promises
Tina:
"Blessed are the peacemakers", means that even when we stand up for justice, there has to be an element of reconciliation, we have to find a way to hear all sides and come up with a reconciling situation.
Jo:
It is so hard when you are up against a system which refuses to hear.
Lesley:
When I came to work at Bethlehem University, a friend rang me. I would be working with Palestinians, but it was important for me to keep my Jewish Israeli friends.
Erdmuthe:
It's so easy to become one-sided. It's important to make links with the Israeli side. And to get to know the many layers on both sides. The Beatitudes may not be addressed to us as individuals, but to the community as a whole.
Tina:
Elias Chacour (a Palestinian priest), said "If you've come here to be pro-Palestinian and anti-Israel, go home. We've had enough divisions. If you've come to be pro-justice, then stay."
Lesley:
Palestinians find it easier to understand the Beatitudes than Christians in the West, because they come from the same background of oppression.

Omar:

To talk about justice, it has to be on the basis of the United Nations resolutions and human rights. If something is wrong, you first have to put it right.

Tina:

I think we should be looking at a higher law than international law.

Over a simple Palestinian lunch, I chatted with Erdmuthe. She had spent three years in England and had enjoyed it, but had left finally because of the intense privacy she found among the English - even among those with whom she was doing a psychology course. However friendly people were on the outside, being invited into people's homes was never part of the deal. Interesting to have an outsider's view of us! She had spent three months as an Ecumenical Accompanier at the Qalandia checkpoint on the road to Ramallah. There was supposed to be a fast-track line for humanitarian workers such as doctors and nurses open for 6am to 8am, but often it was only open for 15 minutes, so Palestinian doctors and patients were often late. Erdmuthe and her colleagues simply had to observe how Palestinians were treated at the checkpoint by the soldiers, and they often felt completely useless. However, later she met a young Israeli who had been a sergeant at that checkpoint, and he told her how much he had hated being observed the whole time. It made her feel that her time on the EAPPI had not been wasted.

She talked about an organisation set up by Israeli feminist mothers called New Profile, trying to change the heavily militarised culture of Israel. For instance, when children are learning numbers in primary school, it is by counting: *"One tank, two rifles, three machine-guns…"*; and at fun fairs children are given the opportunity to practice firing actual weapons. (The New Profile website is in Hebrew, but there is a good Wikipedia article). In 1990 I had bought a postcard in West Jerusalem showing two young women in uniform embracing, with the title "Sorority of fighters". Erdmuthe was going next to the EAPPI at Yanoun - four years after John Howard's tour of duty there.

Erdmuthe left Israel/Palestine in February, *"happy and sad in equal parts"*. In her last letter, she commented about house demolitions, e.g. *"the Tyre school as well as the whole community (in Khan al Ahma) received demolition orders just a few days ago."*

In particular she described watching a man in Qalandia bulldozing his own two-storey house or face security costs of 85,000€.

"The progress is slow, the bulldozer worker needs a lot of breaks, rests his head in his hand as if he cannot believe what he is doing. We stand amongst the neighbours and family and watch. The affected children cry aloud, women and men wipe away tears…"

I could not help being reminded of the Nazi 1942 law by which Jews were not allowed to keep pets, and were not allowed to give them away. They had to kill their own pets themselves. These self-inflicted harms seem to me a most cruel way of breaking the human spirit.

We took a taxi back to the Jaffa gate. The driver was a charming man called Mohammed who spoke very good English. He lives behind the Russian monastery on the Mount of Olives. We walked along Armenian Patriarchate Road to Zion Gate., then out of the Old City to the Dormition Monastery on Mount Zion. This was under Israeli control ever since the 1948 war. Our objective was the Cenacle, meaning Supper Room, a charming Crusader chapel which is meant to mark the spot where Jesus had the last Supper with his disciples. (I think the crypt of St. Mark's Syrian Orthodox Church is a more likely candidate.) From 1524 it was a mosque, but since 1948 it has been under the control Israel's Ministry of the Interior. Christians are allowed to hold services there three times a year. The Thursday service of the Week of Prayer is always held here, an hour earlier than on other evenings.

We got to the Cenacle by climbing the first stairway on the left to a reception area with an attendant on duty, and then into the Cenacle itself. We tried to get there in good time so as to be able to sit down on some stone steps. The Abbey across the lane is inhabited by German Benedictine monks, and it was they who led the service. It was really beautiful, with Taizé chants like Veni, Sancte Spiritus; Bless the Lord, my soul; and Praise to the Lord, the Almighty, the King of Creation sunk in German, French and English. The reading was John 3.1-8, *"Unless one is born of water and the Spirit, one cannot enter the kingdom of God."*

Brother Elias, a German Benedictine monk from the monastery, preached the sermon.
"The Spirit blows where it will.' How can I be born again? How can I pray? We have our doubts, we know our limitations. We are not always full of compassion and kindness. To change our lives, to change our lifestyles, is not easy. When we try to change ourselves, we can change our behaviour for a time,

but not the   heart. After some weeks the former ways will come back.

"When a child is born, it does not have to do very much. The work and the pain is the mother's. The act of being born is somehow passive and inactive. So is being born again. We have to accept our helplessness and poverty. We have to live in the wind of the Spirit, in the Gospel, In the love of Christ. We cannot entirely change our state of mind, but we are able to realise that, despite our smallness, our weakness, we are simple creatures, but loved by God. And within this deep love, we can, not only change, but also and above all, be transformed."

After the sermon came the prayers. When the Lord's Prayer was said, each in their own language, the echoes around the arched ceiling were very moving.

Afterwards we were invited to the Monastery refectory, where we had the simple and delicious Palestinian snack of sesame bread, oil and za'atar, an utterly typical Palestinian mix of herbs like oregano, basil, thyme and caraway seeds.

Leaving the crush, Jo and I made our way into the church - built in 1906 by German Benedictines - very impressive. We spent some time there, looking at all the mosaics. We then made our way into the the crypt where there is a statue of the Virgin Mary sleeping in death , hence the name of the church, the Dormition.

I celebrated Christmas here in 1963 when I attended the midnight mass. The church was full, mostly of Israelis, and the sermon was in Hebrew and English. Apparently Christmas day is still a time when Israeli Jews feel free to go into a church service. I was accompanied by four fellow Masada volunteers - Christians were allowed to leave one day early. We were two English nurses, an elderly lady from San Francisco and a young Swedish man who carried two live scorpions with him. After the Midnight Mass we had a very quiet celebration of our own in the girls' dormitory consisting of nuts, fruitcake and Dubonnet.

We got back to our hotel before torrential rain hit the City. But the kitchens were shut, so we had to brave the rain and go to the Gloria for supper. Afterwards I had a drink at the bar and was invited to join a group of ten Greek young people who were there on pilgrimage. They were gathered round an Abuna - Father - who was a monk at Mar Saba, an ancient and remote monastery, founded in the 5th century, clinging to one side of the Kidron ravine in the Judaean desert. About 20 monks live there. They treated him with great respect. All his movements were slow and considered. But his mind was clearly incisive and he had a great sense of humour.

FRIDAY 27th JANUARY

THE OTHER ISRAEL

Today I went to visit a friend in Tel Aviv, Mary-Clare. When I was a curate in Streatham in the mid-80's, I knew her mother, Julia Adam, a former concert pianist and a faithful member of St Leonard's. I met Mary-Clare on one of her visits to London and we became friends. In 1990 I visited Israel again and we travelled round Galilee, meeting the charismatic Palestinian priest Elias Chacour in the village of Ibillin. We had kept in touch ever since. She had visited Linda and me a few times in England and now I could return the visit.

The torrential rain of the night before had settled down to a persistent drizzle as I walked past the city walls along Jaffa Road with the Dormition Monastery in the distance. Between 1948 and 1967 this had been no man's land between the conflicting sides. Now it is a four lane highway with underpasses.

I put 60 agurot in the ticket machine and travelled on the Jerusalem Light Rail to the West Jerusalem Bus Station. What

a culture shock! Brash, noisy, and very Jewish. Loads of soldiers, going off on their tours of duty. And the guns! Taken as simply a matter of course. I had a coffee and a savoury bread roll as my breakfast.

English is often a passport to making contact in many cities of the world, but I did not find it so here. You really have to speak, and read, Hebrew.

I went through the forbidding security doors and got the 9.00 bus to Tel Aviv, driving through the steady rain, with the top of the Harp Bridge lost in the cloud. A really wintry scene.
As soon as we came off the Judaean Hills, the weather

cleared and we had lovely sunshine. Mary Clare had told me to get bus 18 from the bus station when I arrived - a surprisingly primitive and muddy bus station for a modern city. I could not find bus 18, so I took one in the vague general direction of her

address. Later I found that my bus had terminated at different bus station. As we drove through Tel Aviv, noticed a gay bookshop - much more open here than in Jerusalem. When thought I was near I went on foot and found a splendid example of

Bauhaus architecture, unfortunately in the wrong direction. I walked back and eventually took a taxi which drove 200 yards and landed me outside Mary-Clare's apartment.

I got into the lift , finding to my surprise that the door of the lift was actually the front door of the flat. I pushed it open and encountered an utterly Tel Aviv moment. I

was blest by fantastic live music of piano, violin and cello playing a Trio by Pizzaiaola,the famous Tango composer. I

was of course rather later than I should have been, so I had missed the Mozart and Schumann.

Mary-Clare's father, Leonhard Adam, was a Jew from Berlin and a distinguished expert in art and anthropology. He came to England in the 1930's. In 1939 he wrote an excellent book for Pelican on "Primitive Art" (still available from Amazon for 1p.) which was published in 1940, the same year that he was deported to Australia as "a friendly enemy alien". Mary-Clare shared the same fascination with these cultures and lived in Papua-New Guinea between1974 and 1979.

Moshe Murvitz was first violin in the Israel Philharmonic as well as having an international career, which is how he met Mary-Clare. She joined him in 1984. He was fiercely anti-Zionist. Once Mary-Clare mentioned the splendid stone house in Yafo where friends of theirs lived. Moshe responded by saying he would never live in a house from which the original inhabitants had been evicted. Similarly he said he would never, ever go to the West Bank as a *"conqueror"*, only as an *"invited guest."*

He died from cancer a few years ago. Mary-Clare remarried Giora Bernstein, a charming man, also a violinist and conductor. He was born in Vienna as Georg but left to stay with his grandparents in Czechoslovakia after Hitler's takeover of Austria in 1938. When the Nazis invaded Czechoslovakia in 1939 they urged him to leave, which is when he came to Palestine,and took the name Giora - Georg was not a very good name at that time. His grandparents both died in Treblinka concentration camp.

Mary-Clare's daughter Batia is a highly talented concert pianist and so continues the family tradition.

Mary-Clare is a Christian. In 1990 she introduced me to the church Abu Ghosh, with its beautiful singing, where I also met the British ambassador. Because of her time in the Pacific, she is now honorary Israeli Consul for the Solomon Islands. She told me that in 1990 Israel decided to welcome Russian Jews into the country provided just one set of grandparent had been Jewish. The unexpected result was an influx of Russian Christians, and now the local Greek Orthodox churches are full!

Mary-Clare has urged me to take on a holiday chaplaincy at Paphos, Cyprus, where she often goes. There she met a 6 year old Filipino girl with an advanced brain tumour. Only two hospitals in the world were equipped to treat it, one in the U.S.A. and the other in Israel. Mary-Claire said she would be the girl's contact person in Israel, so she had her operation in Tel Aviv. In the ICU the girl had a vision of angel, and annoyed others in the ward by singing Christmas carols! She lived a further seven years, dying at the age of 13.

Giora was going to hospital to prepare for a heart operation, (the operation was successful), and he dropped me on his way at the Tel Aviv Museum of Art. This is an astonishing building, with its  enormous front plaza and entrance hall and wonderful collection of impressionists and post-impressionists.

I was engrossed by two Chagalls, "Solitude" (1933), and the Wailing Wall (1932), which shows what it was like before 1967 or indeed 1948.

A painting of Ein Karem (1928), gives an idyllic picture of a Palestinain village in British Mandate Palestine.It is now a rather arty village on the western outskirts of

Jerusalem with several churches linked allegedly to the parents of John the Baptist. The local Palestinians fled in 1948 and were replaced by Jews from Morocco and Romania.

From there it was a half hour's walk through light drizzle to the former bus station. I passed a small tent city where homeless people lived. I asked a passer-by who they were; he thought they might be homeless Sudanese refugees. In fact they were ordinary Israelis, caught up in the extortionate cost of housing in Israel. In 2016 there had been  a mass demonstration of people sleeping out to protest at the high cost of housing in Tel Aviv. I remembered what the couple from Highgate in the plane coming over had said about helping the homeless in Tel Aviv.

 I joined the queue at the bus station and I learnt that the municipality is planning to build a proper modern bus station.

As the bus travelled across the fertile plain I could not help wondering how much of this land would have been owned by Palestinian families before 1948.

Back in rainy Jerusalem I got the Light Rail back to the corner of the Jaffa Road, and walked down past Jaffa Gate to have a late lunch of shawarma and salad in a small restaurant on the Greek Patriarchate Road. There I met Linda, a Canadian and a born adventurer. She had come from Hanoi, Vietnam where she had lived for 19 years. I told her about the Week of Prayer for Christian Unity and asked if she would like to come with me to the Coptic Church for the 5.00 service, and she said she would. We walked through heavy rain up towards the rooftop monastery of the Ethiopians to the Coptic Church beyond.

St Anthony's Coptic Orthodox Church was, as always, beautifully if rather gaudily decorated, and well lit - for some

of the time. Twice the service all the lights failed. It did not faze anyone and it did not stop the singing by the fine ladies' choir. The service simply continued without hesitation in total darkness. Later I asked if the torrential rain had caused a power failure, but I was told, no. It was because switching on all the lights of the chandeliers had overloaded the fuse board!

The service was held jointly between the Coptic and Syrian

Orthodox churches. The languages were Coptic and Arabic. (Coptic had been the normal language of Egyptians until the 13th century when it was made illegal). The Gospel was in Arabic and English, and was part of the story of the shepherds at Christmas (Luke 2.8-14). Then came this prayer, in English.

> *"Triune God, you reveal yourself to us as Father and Creator, as Son and Saviour, and as Spirit and Giver of Life, and yet you are one. You break through our human boundaries and renew us. Give us a new heart to overcome all that endangers our unity in you. We pray in the name of Jesus Christ by the power of the Holy Spirit. Amen.*

Then came the sermon, in Arabic, with a translation into English on the back of the order of service. Here is how it ended:

"Dear guests let's leave this negative speech and the words of despair which say most of our times. we should know that there is one truth which is the history which mentioned a lot for the events that led to the misunderstanding of the accurate meaning of the theological words in some occasions which led to the division*. But in this era we hope to reach the unity of the church and we insistonit.

There were a lot of meetings that were full of joy, hope and peace between pope Tawadros the second and pope Francis . The meeting of pope of Vatican with Ecumenical patriarch in Jerusalem. the meeting of the patriarch of Russia and the pope of Rome. Agreements between the Lutheran church and Vatican. (the gates of heades shall not prevail against it) . Neither the devil nor the divisions, this church as established by Jesus. it was built on the rock.

Finally, we should pray not just in this week but all the time for the unity of the church. Till someday this desired unity comes soon. Thank you all."

(*This refers to a theological split that occurred as a result of the Council of Chalcedon AD 451. The issue was whether Jesus had two natures divine and human, or one combined nature, or a divine nature with the human nature being a kind of play-acting etc. The churches on all sides have now come to accept that the split was all about a linguistic misunderstanding).

Then came sharing the kiss of peace with one another, the Lord's Prayer each in our own language, and the blessing from all the heads of the churches present.

Afterwards there was a lively reception in the Big Hall of the monastery - which was not very big. There was squash and biscuits, and coffee brought by an imperturbable man holding the tray of drinks one-handed above our heads as he squeezed through the jostling crowd.

I chatted to Ninos, or Nikos, the Greek dentist whom Linda and I had met in the 2012 Week of Prayer. I told him of my plan

to go to Bethlehem the following day. The Jewish sabbath had started at 4.00 on Friday. I knew from previous experience that West Jerusalem would be completely quiet on the sabbath, so to go to Bethlehem was an obvious destination. I went home through the rain-swept streets.

I had supper on my own, then out of curiosity switched on the TV to see what was on Israeli television on the Sabbath. The answer was "12 Years a Slave", Anchorman 2", and "Viaduc" a French film about a disaffected teenager.

A Note: The first reading in the service was Genesis 17.1-8, in Arabic. Later I found out it was God's promise to Abraham: *"The whole land of Canaan, where you are now an alien, I will give as an everlasting possession to you and your descendants after you, and I will be their God."* (Genesis 17.8)
What do we do with that?

I have an article on this contentious question called "Israel and the Bible - an Investigation. It can be downloaded from the links page of my website www.bibleinbrief.org.

The Lord's Prayer in Aramiac and Hebrew

Pater Noster Church

Corridor in the Knigthts Palace Hotel

Breakfast at the Knights Palace

SATURDAY 28th JANUARY

AN UPSETTING DAY

I woke up to a cold rainy day and no breakfast. Eventually I made my way to the East Jerusalem bus station and found the bus to Bethlehem. The bus was quite full with a mixture of tourists and Palestinians. I sat next to a family from Guanchou in China. The weather did not improve as we went up towards Bethlehem. Indeed there was snow lying on the hillside. At the security checkpoint soldiers came onto the bus and checked our passports. I was in some consternation when we got to Bethlehem, because the bus did not go to the central bus station, but dropped us on a side street 10 minutes' walk

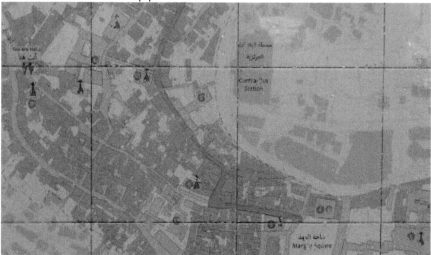

up to the city centre. Apparently the bus station had been separated from the rest of Bethlehem by the Separation Wall cutting the town in half. See the town map above.

Not knowing quite where we were made us anxious, and the incessant rain also dampened our spirits. The main street was rather depressing anyhow with the lack of tourists and the economic stranglehold of the occupation. I found my way to the Evangelical Lutheran Centre, which I had discovered previously as an oasis. Here I had a welcome hot chocolate

and talked with the young woman, Mirna, who was the receptionist. She said,

"All has been taken, they took many lands. They wanted to take the Cremisan vineyards for the Wall, but the churches together fought for it. The vineyards are owned *by the Don Bosco order (and make very good wine indeed). If I want to go to Jerusalem, I need to apply for a visa seven days in advance. We are in prison here."*

I asked if I could take her picture , but she said no, so here is one of me at the Lutheran Centre.

I carried on down Pope Paul VI Street and stopped at the small St Mary's Syrian Orthodox Church. I told the caretaker that I had been at the Syrian Orthodox service the evening before. It is a beautiful little church, but, chatting to the caretaker, I felt the sadness of a dwindling community. And of course there is the tragic history behind it.

At the entrance of the church is a painted board showing the martyrdom of Armenians and Syrian Orthodox during the Armenian genocide. The one wearing a hat is Armenian, those with crosses on their hoods are Syrian Orthodox.

See Appendix 1 for a description of the Armenian Genocide, and a reaction from the churches here.

In Manger Square I went to the Bethlehem Information Centre, a rather sad place. It was interesting to see a scale model of Bethlehem, and photos of the village round about 1900. The Church of the Nativity is in front of the open ground in the foreground.

I was now both cold and hungry so I went to a restaurant on Manger Square and had lentil soup.

Then on to the church of the Nativity, bending to enter the tiny entrance, aptly named the Door of Humility. It was one of the few churches to escape destruction during the Persian invasion of 614, perhaps because of statues of the magi or wise men, whom the Persians would have recognised as their own. You can still see the floor mosaics from Constantine's church, c.330. However, the church had been destroyed in a revolt by the Samaritans in the 6th century, so it now stands

is largely what was built in the 6th century by the emperor Justinian. It was full of the scaffolding as a major restoration of the interior was going on when I went, with the hope that it would be completed in six months. A shame, because I could not see the marvellous Byzantine mosaics.

Underneath the church is a rabbit warren of caves and grottoes, one of which is traditionally identified as the spot where Jesus was born. It is certainly more authentic than any number of Nativity paintings and Christmas cards. We are told in Luke 2 that Mary gave birth in a stable because there was no room at the inn. In fact, the word for "inn" is exactly the same as the "upper room" where Jesus had the Last Supper with his disciples. A standard Palestinian dwelling was an upper floor, just above ground level where all daily living took place, with a cave underneath for the animals in winter. This is where Mary had Jesus

because it was the most private place they had.

I went down the steep steps, and spent quite a long time sitting quietly at the back of the underground chapel as that was the most peaceful option. I was somewhat distressed by the crowds of pilgrims, of all nationalities, crowding into the tiny space, not, mostly, to pray, but to take flash photos.

I walked back along the ridge on which Bethlehem is built - half an hour of hard walking, and caught the bus for the hour's journey back to Jerusalem.

From Damascus Gate I walked up Salah ed-Din Street, East Jerusalem, to the Educational Bookshop where I had arranged to meet Jo and Lesley. Nablus Road was not particularly pretty, but clearly much more economically vibrant than Bethlehem.

The Educational Bookshop is tiny but full of fascinating books about Palestine, with a small cafe upstairs. To my surprise Jo and Lesley wee already there. I was tempted to buy "Gaza Unsilenced" but being rather cowardly I did not - I knew I would find it too upsetting. Anyone of a weak disposition should steer clear of any curiosity about the dreadful conditions of the people in Gaza, which the U.N. has declared will be unliveable in within three years.

I went off with Jo and Lesley to visit an old friend and colleague of theirs, Betty Majaj. On the way we stopped at a small general shop and bought one of the two main Israeli newspapers, Ha'aretz.

Here are front page headlines on Friday 27th January:

Poised for PM's fall,politicians fight over spoils
As law closes in, Netanyahu feels right-wing pressure
for big moves in West Bank
PM's story apparently doesn't match Milchan's, which
could spell his doom.
Israel's risky embrace of Trump
Public security minister moves to decriminalise
marijuana use
Israel scrambling to explain failure on its Kotel vows
       (i.e. Why has the government still not set aside

part of the Western Wall for equal access by both men and women)

Note: There are more extended quotes from Israeli newspapers in Appendix 2.

 We walked to the house of Betty Majaj, an indomitable old lady of 90 who had only retired four years previously at the age of 86, and with whom both Jo and Lesley had worked. She had been born in 1926 in Beirut, Lebanon under the French mandate. Against the wishes of her family she undertook nursing training at the American University of Beirut (AUB). In her last year there, on the paediatric ward, she worked with Amin, a young Palestinian doctor from Jerusalem, and they fell in love with each other. Overcoming their families' objections they were married in June 1947, and after a honeymoon in a luxury hotel in Beirut, went back to Jerusalem to start their new life together, where they were part of the congregation of St George's Anglican Cathedral. Betty still lives in the same house as they had then. Amin started a paediatric clinic in West Jerusalem. With the outbreak of war in 1948, Betty and the women of the family made the long and dangerous drive to Beirut, while Amin set up a new hospital in Bethany dealing with the many war wounded as well as ordinary medical emergencies. Betty came back despite the risks and used her nursing training to cope with all the demands. Nine month later the little hospital was moved to the Augusta Victoria. Over the next twenty years a new children's ward was established and Amin conducted world-class research into the effect of vitamin deficiencies in children. Betty went to work in the children's ward, first as assistant

matron and then as matron. She gave it up in 1955 when she became pregnant. Eventually she had three daughters and a son. The 1967 war was another disaster, with a second refugee crisis, families split up again, and the children's ward in the Augusta Victoria destroyed by Israeli artillery. Amin did not have the heart thereafter to go back to his research. Then in 1975 civil war erupted in Lebanon, and Betty's family saw their whole way of life destroyed. Betty made frequent trips there to support them. The appalling conditions were made worse when Israel joined the war in 1982. All the Christian towns east of Sidon were destroyed. The war lasted till 1990 and between 130,000 and 250,000 civilians were killed. Almost a million people became refugees.

In 1966 a centre had been established to provide medical and rehabilitation services for children with physical disabilities, called the Princess Basma Centre because of the support from the Jordanian royal family. After 1967 that support was gone, and the Lutheran World Federation took the Centre under its wing. In 1983, after almost 30 years working as a mother, Betty was asked to become the new Director of the Centre. *"I did feel it an honour to serve my community as a whole, and those with disabilities in particular. It was an opportunity to serve."*

Betty set about expanding the Centre, and doing the fundraising herself to make it happen. Children were welcomed who had a wide range of disabilities, such as cerebral palsy and congenital deformities. She set about creating a network of locally qualified staff; Lesley's work at the Bethlehem University was key to this, and Jo helped organise the work placements, following on from her Quaker placement as Betty's admin assistant. In 1987 Betty started a school for the children, the same year as the intifada started, adding a new floor and a new year grade each academic year until they got their first high school class in 2010. By 1992 a professional multidisciplinary tam for the centre was in place. In 2000 the name was changed to "The Jerusalem Princess Basma Centre for Disabled Children." Betty finally retired in 2012 at the age of 86, though she still helps out on the board of directors and as a volunteer when needed.

This was the remarkable person who had invited us to tea, with a

splendid array of quiche, chocolate cake, German stollen and an electric teapot! Jo, Lesley and Betty caught up with each others' mutual friends. Betty's eldest daughter Lina was with us. She is the P.A. to the present Director of the Princess Basma, but her special love is writing icons (You write icons, you don't paint them). Her favourite icon is the one of Christ as Pantocrator, or Ruler of the Universe, seen in the photo.

While reflecting on her life' including the suffering of three wars, Betty said to us, "I will keep patience whatever happens."

From Betty's house we took a taxi to the Ethiopian Orthodox Church, the only church we visited in West Jerusalem.
It is a completely circular church, with an ambulatory (means walking round and round) round the walls of the sanctuary. Ideal for a hot Israel summer, but always cold in January.

The service of Vespers had haunting and beautiful music, with various

processions emerging from the sanctuary into the place of the people, sometimes with ceremonial umbrellas. The service was shared with the Syrian and Armenian churches. The service was in Amharic and Arabic and Armenian. The Old Testament reading was in English from the prophet Micah, highly appropriate for the current situation:

"Out of Zion will go forth the law,
and the word of the LORD from Jerusalem.
He shall judge between many peoples
and shall decide for strong nations far off;
and they shall beat their swords into ploughshares
and their spears into pruning hooks;
nation shall not lift up sword against nation,
neither shall they learn war any more;
but they shall sit every man under his vine
and under his fig tree,
and none shall make them afraid;
for the mouth of the LORD has spoken.

(Micah 4.2-4)

The priest of the church, Aba Flssiha Tsion, said, *"Peace is necessary for the whole world. Without peace it is difficult to take an initiative. We are praying God to grant us peace, full peace, in the world and in our own lives".*

Afterwards we walked across the courtyard for refreshments and the traditional drumming, singing and dancing, an energetic rendering of psalms of praise, which is one of the glories of the Ethiopian church.

Jo and I walked back to the Old City to the Armenian quarter, where we were meeting Lesley and Bassam and his wife Wafa' at the well known restaurant Bulghourji for an Armenian feast. Bassam was charming and well-informed   It was here that he told me that I had bought the necklace for my wife from a well-known cheat!

We got back to our hotel at 10.00.

SUNDAY 29th JANUARY

UNITY IN THE SPIRIT

We got up in a relaxed way and all three of us went to Christ Church for their 9.30 service.

There are two Anglican churches in Jerusalem and they have the reputation of not being on speaking terms. Christ Church was consecrated in 1849 with a commitment to the Jewish people. The interior was kept as plain as possible. Only in 1948 was a wooden cross placed on the Lord's table to stop Jordanian solders mistaking it for a synagogue. In 1996 I had gone to the evening service and happened to sit next to a churchwarden. I asked him about the opening of the Christian bookshop in the compound which I had attended that week, and I commented that it was a shame that the bishop had not been invited. The churchwarden said they had discussed it at length, but in the end decided not to invite him as he would have just taken over. I thought, that's true!

I was interested to see that there are services in Hebrew on Monday evening and on the Shabat, and a study group in Arabic on Friday evening. All other services are in English.

I found the service excellent, and I coped with the length - two and a quarter hours. The notices came at the beginning with a list of meetings in English, Hebrew and Arabic, and an update on one of their church workers, Andrew Bruton, who had been arrested in Turkey three months ago and still had not been charged or released. There was sensitive worship music to begin. The liturgy included a number of passages from the psalms, e.g. Psalm 51 for the confession. The Sh'ma was said by everyone: *"Hear, O Israel, the Lord is our God the Lord alone..."* The Sanctus, (Holy, holy, holy) was sung in Hebrew - very appropriate because it was originally a synagogue prayer. The word Messiah rather than Christ is used - again appropriate, the Hebrew word rather than the Greek word, both meaning 'The Anointed One".

Then came the readings. Christ Church chooses its own readings. They were embarking on a series on Matthew, with all of February dedicated to Matthew 5 with Matthew 6 on fasting on Ash Wednesday. Last Sunday they had read about the start of Jesus' ministry in Matthew 4. This morning they were reading Matthew 5.1-12, the Beatitudes, so we heard it for the fourth time in one week! Perhaps we were being told to pay attention to it. The other two readings were Micah 6.1-8 and 1 Corinthians 1.18-31

David Pileggi is the rector, appointed in 2008, but he was on the staff of Christ Church for the previous 18 years organising the Shoresh Study Tours. Here is most of what he said about the Beatitudes:

"Last Sunday we talked about Jesus initiating his ministry, and how he connected repentance with the kingdom of God. They go together like bacon and eggs or ham and cheese. Repentance is not something we do once. We do it throughout our lives. And we drew the connection between repentance, the kingdom of God and healing.

"We're now in chapter 5, and we hear the words of Jesus. His words are challenging, but they can also be healing.

"The problem with our text today is that it is subject to discussion and disagreement going back to the earliest church of Origen and Augustine. Is this for everybody? Is it just good ethical advice for the whole world? Or are these not for the world itself, are these words for Christians, for all Christians? Or are they for the initiated, the Marine Corps, the S.A.S in our midst? Are they even doable? Or are they impossible to do, as Martin Luther thought?

"I would say that without a proper understanding of the Jewish context in which it was written, it is easy to go astray. Jesus stands on two pillars. The first is the message of the kingdom of heaven. The second is discipleship. And here they overlap one another. We have to be clear. What does it mean to be a disciple of Jesus, and what does the kingdom of heaven mean?

Whether it is the kingdom of God in the synoptic gospels, or eternal life in John, or being in Christ in Paul, they all point to one thing, to a present reality, to God's presence in our lives today, and to God's power now.

Is the kingdom of God present or future? It doesn't work that way in Hebrew. Hebrew is not a very precise language. You don't want to send someone to the moon using Hebrew. But do you want to recite poetry in Hebrew? Absolutely! In Hebrew the kingdom of heaven means more than one thing. It can mean God's powerful presence in in our lives. And when his power is present, he is bringing healing, he is bringing blessing.

It is also a people. It is as if God says, this is the name I'm giving my community. Those people who are submitting themselves to me, who accept my authority. The question is, have we been obedient to his commandments? Those people who have done so, Jesus calls the kingdom of heaven. The issue is not whether we are going to heaven, The issue is whether he is reigning over us, is God present in our lives?

Matthew 5.1-3. Here you have the crowd and the disciples. Who is he talking to? Over the years I've been convinced that he is talking to the disciples, to those people who are willing to give everything. These ideas only work in the context of obedience, of a lifestyle of repentance, of continued faith in Jesus himself. Where is God ruling and reigning? It's in the community where Jesus is king.

To be in the kingdom community you have to be poor in spirit. We usually come to this after serious trouble. It might be bankruptcy or prison. It's amazing how many people find the Lord after trouble of one kind or another. These are the people whom God is ruling and reigning over.

The seven other beatitudes tell us what it means to be poor in spirit.

"Blessed are those who mourn." It's not just a question of personal tragedy. it includes being heart-broken about what might be happening in the nation.

"Blessed are those who hunger and thirst after righteousness." It means longing for righteousness in our community.

"Blessed are the merciful." It means that because we have not got it together, we will show mercy to others who have not got it together.

"Blessed are the pure in heart." It means those who seek and desire purity in a moral sense, including sexual morality.

"Blessed are the peacemakers" - those who actively work for reconciliation, who build bridges.

We enter the kingdom of heaven through repentance, but we stay in the place where God can rule over our lives and bring us blessings by being broken, being poor in spirit.

Finally, I want to remind everyone that Jesus is the Messiah who blesses. God's intention for the whole human family from the beginning was to bring us blessing. In the midst of suffering, loss, self-denial, there are incredible blessings.

"Blessed are the meek," it might mean those who are powerless. Still, in God's understanding, and in eternity, this really is the community that counts."

We went up to kneel at the rail for communion. When David came to Lesley, he gave her the bread by name. He recognised her from a study group they were both in 27 years before!

Everyone went out into the courtyard for coffee and refreshments. After some time I was able to speak to David Pillegi, because I wanted to ask him about relationships with St George's. He said, *"We have a good relationship with Bishop Suheli, and especially with Dean Hosam. We don't hobnob, but we have good personal relations. The previous two bishops were crooks."*

I met a very sad young Palestinian man, a member of the church. He came from Gaza and was very concerned about his sister who was still there. He gave me a rosary, which I still have. Christ Church has an excellent website: christchurchjerusalem.org.

I went round to pay my respects to St Mark's Syrian Orthodox Church again, but it was locked. On the way I met a young haredi, a religious Jew with black hat, side curls, black suit, open white shirt etc. I asked him if he spoke English. He said, no, he only spoke Yiddish. He was clearly from an ultra-orthodox group who believe that Hebrew is a sacred language and should not be used for everyday purposes. So they still speak yiddish, the language of East European Jewry. For instance, the word for synagogue is "Shul", like the German for "Schule". It reminded me of a visit to Mea

Shearim in 1975. This is an ultra-orthodox area of West Jerusalem, settled by Eastern European religious Jews in 1874, the first Jewish settlement outside the Old City. They are (or were) against the state of Israel, as the true Israel can only be founded by the Messiah. I saw a graffiti: ZIONISM

IS BLASPHEMY. It is the only part of Israel where people regularly used to display the PLO flag. This was the standard response of religious Jews up to the Six Day War. The speed and thoroughness of Israel's victory (becuse of a pre-emptive strike which destroyed the Egyptian airforce) convinced them that God was indeed in this thing, and religious Jews are now probably the most fervent supporters of the state of Israel and of the policy of building settlements on the West Bank.

I walked down to Haddad Street with religious Jews striding towards the Jewish Quarter. I found them very hard to approach: *"Do you speak English?"* *"No."* I found the steps up to the rooftop promenade. This is like a first floor street, linking the Jewish and Muslim Quarters, like a completely separate village, rather untidy, dirty - completely unlike the Jewish Quarter proper. It seems to be inhabited solely by haredis, the religious ultra-orthodox.

When I got to the Rooftop Promenade, I saw a large group of Israeli soldiers. I asked one of them what this was about. They were a group of soldiers stationed at Eilat. They had come to Jerusalem on a day out to have a tour of Jerusalem. I did not ask why they had come in their uniforms. I note that 5 were religious Jews, wearing the kippa, 20 were secular, without a kippa.

A few minutes later I got into a conversation with two young soldiers, who clearly liked each other. They were both stationed at Ashkelon, 15 miles from the northern boundary of the Gaza Strip. Andrea, the man, had three years of duty to go. He came from a village near Haifa. He was responsible for Combat Life and Safety. I asked if he meant Health and Safety. No, he said, it was Life and Safety, for instance with demolished houses.

Tal came from a settlement in northern Israel and had 2 years 8 months to go before her tour of duty ended. *"You could be a mother by then,"* I joked, only to be met by expressions of complete bafflement. They suggested that I went to Mahane Yehuda market in West Jerusalem for lunch, a suggestion I was very pleased to follow.

I walked through the Damascus Gate to up to the Jaffa Road where I got the Light Rail to Mahane Yehuda. It is a bustling, thriving place where you can buy local produce and exotic spices. It has two market streets, a covered market and an open-air market. When I went it was pretty dirty with piles of rubbish bags littering the streets, due, I was told, to a strike by refuse collectors. I found a fish restaurant and had sea bass, chips and six side salads for 75 NIS. What was wonderful was to have a real fresh wholemeal roll. After a week of Palestinian pitta bread, familiar yeasted bread tastes out of this world!

Going back to the hotel, I met Jo, Lesley and Bassam at an Armenian merchant's opposite the hotel entrance.

The owner was George Sandrouni, and an old friend of Jo and Lesley's. He made beautiful authentic Armenian pottery. He drew the outlines himself, and his daughters coloured them in. Each piece took between 25 and 30 hours' work. I am pretty hard to sell to, but I bought a fine wall tile with a red Jerusalem cross. I was now uncertain about the necklace I had bought for Linda, and I wanted to buy her a pendant made of Roman glass, like the one that had been stolen two years before. George advised where to go for good jewellery. George has a wonderful website: sandrouni.com, in which all the stages of making a design are shown.

I went off to Christian Quarter Road. I could not find the shop I had been to previously, but found another good one called Tamara, owned by a man called Mohammed. I happily made my purchase, and then he took me to meet his English wife who had just started a small art gallery with some lovely modern paintings round the corner in Aqabat al-Khanqa St. He then got a young relation to  take me to another shop where I would get a good deal on some more jewellery. This is absolutely standard practice. Be prepared! But this time I was adamant.

Then up to the Greek Melkite Catholic Cathedral of Our Lady of the Annunciation. It was in Greek Catholic Patriarchate Road, between our hotel and Jaffa Gate. The Melkite or Greek Catholic Church dates itself from the earliest Christian community in Jerusalem. 1724 marked the decisive split between the Greek Orthodox Church in the Middle East and the Greek Catholic Church. Briefly, they are Catholics who use the Byzantine liturgy and keep the other Orthodox traditions but acknowledge the primacy of the Pope. They are principally based round Syria and Palestine. There are 1.6 million Melkite Christians world-wide. The official language is Arabic.

The church is very fine, everything is either painted of gilded. The service was mostly in Arabic, but the whole service was translated into English. The readings were Micah 4.1-5 (in English), Revelation 21.1-5 (in French) and John 20.11-18 (sung in Arabic). Archbishop Joseph-Jules Zehry radiated good humour and love for those around him. He gave an impassioned sermon, in Arabic, pleading for unity, but helpfully provided an English translation, of which this is an extract:

"Although the Greek Melkite Catholic Church entered into full communion with the Catholic Church since 1724, She has not left her elder sister but continues to follow the same liturgy, rites and feasts according to the Eastern Byzantine Christian tradition. In prayer, we ask the Lord that the full unity with the beloved sister Greek Orthodox Church be re-established. In this holy church, I personally raise my daily prayer for His Beatitude Patriarch Theophilos and my brothers of Orthodox, Anglican

and Lutheran Churches as well as my brothers Bishops of the Catholic Churches....

"The first reading from the Book of Micah speaks to us about the Mount: Mount Zion on top of which is built the holy City... To it will run the peoples of the earth and they will learn the Law of the Lord. Of their swords they shall make tools to cultivate the the land, and of their spears they will make sickles, and they shall learn no more war.

"What was foreseen by Micah the Prophet has been realised in the coming of Christ the Lord, the Word of God who was incarnate and born of the Virgin Mary, our mother. Her faith in the annunciation by the archangel Gabriel opened the door of salvation to all humanity.. This is why we thank her and venerate her in our prayers....

"My beloved brethren, We all, who live in this holy city surrounded by its great walls and marked by its holy places, witness to the Divine salvation which took place here. The Cenacle where the Last Supper took place, and from Gethsemane to Caiaphas' palace then to Pilate's palace where Christ was condemned to be crucified and taken carrying His cross to Golgotha, the tomb where Christ's body was buried from which he rose after three days. How beautiful and sacred is this holy city. However, we heard in the second reading (Revelation 21.1-5) of "The New Jerusalem coming down out if heaven from God". This new Jerusalem is much larger than this holy city we see on earth. It is larger than the universe.... This is the Church, the "bride of Christ"... All those who *believed in the passion, death and Resurrection of Christ, and went on preaching with all their power and love of Christ and their faith in the Resurrection; but also who suffered or were martyred for the sake of Christ enter in their white garments this holy city, "holy Jerusalem" coming down from heaven.*

"My prayer today is for us to reconcile with each other quickly as Christ reconciled us. Let us embrace each other and reconcile with each other starting from this holy city so that our reconciliation and unity may be a "a spring of life-giving water"...

At the end of the service came the "artoclasia" or "breaking of the bread" as an Agape or love-feast. Loaves of bread were carried ceremoniously around the church, and brought to the front. After the blessing everyone was invited to receive a piece of the blessed bread dipped in wine, a fine conclusion to the Week of Prayer for Christian Unity.

Afterwards there was food and drink in the hall outside the church. I met up again with Nino the Greek dentist and with Ken of the white beard, the American carpenter who had lived 23 years in Jerusalem. Ken talked enthusiastically about Vassula Rydén. She is Greek Orthodox born in Cairo. Now

in her 70's she lives in Switzerland. On 20th September 1986 she started receiving messages from Jesus and the Virgin Mary through a type of automatic writing, and received over 2,000 messages up to 2003. Her writings call for people to "repent, love God, and unify the churches". Her first message was:

'I am the Light and I shine for everybody to see; have no fear, My Path is straight; My Path will lead you to Me; I will meet you and you will recognise Me, for I radiate Peace and Love".

Some monks in the monastery where I go on retreat rate her very highly. However, the hierarchies of the Catholic and Orthodox churches do not believe she is divinely inspired. But Ken is impressed. She brings clergy together from all the churches, 700 in one conference. To him she has made unity a reality.

Back to the hotel for supper at 7.00, to the Gloria Hotel for coffee and arak, and then packing.

MONDAY 30th JANUARY

DEPARTURE

Our flight was not till the afternoon, so we had a couple of hours free after breakfast. I made my way down to the Church of the Holy Sepulchre at 9.00 and was delighted to find that the chapel of Calvary was entirely empty, so I could pray there undisturbed for 15 minutes. What a privileged way to say farewell to Jerusalem.

I then made my way back up Franciscan Road and as I sat and had a fresh orange juice, saw George Sandrinou and Ninos come out on the street. It was very funny, hearing the banter between these two Jerusalem alpha males, Armenian and Greek. One of the jokes that George recounted was about an argument between a Greek and an Italian as to which of their two countries had made the most cultural impact:

Greek:	*We discovered art!*
Italian:	*We discovered architecture!*
Greek :	*We invented maths!*
Italian:	*We invented music!*
Greek:	*We discovered sex!*
Italian:	*And we discovered how to do it with women!*

Just opposite was a small gift shop that I had not been in before. In fact it was a remarkable place, Melia Art and Training Centre, created by the Arab Orthodox Society. Many of the women in West Bank villages made their living through selling vegetables and handicrafts on the streets of Jerusalem. In the 1990s Israel refused to allow anything from the West Bank to be sold in Jerusalem, leading to great impoverishment. Melia provides a market for those who cannot physically reach Jerusalem to sell their crafts, and the training project helps establish social networks to keep women connected and supporting each other. The traditional Palestinian embroidery is beautiful. They have a website: meliaartandtrainingcenter.com.

Bassam drove the three of us to the airport and we arrived in plenty of time. I thought that that was the end of my Israel experience, but no! Going down the ramp towards the departure lounge was a series of 22 panels celebrating the history of Zionism from 1897 to the present. It was very well done, and very one-sided. In Appendix 4 I lay out all the text of the panels, but with notes about other narratives which should be heard.

For instance, in the panel next to Israel and the Diaspora, a photo shows primary schoolgirls standing around a large floor map of Israel, in which there is no West Bank and no Gaza Strip! Anyone for the 2-state solution?

We spent a quiet three hours in the departure lounge, during which I bought the two main daily newspapers in Israel, Ha'aretz and the Jerusalem Post and was then called to the plane. I relate what was in them, a snapshot of normal Israeli political life, in Appendix 2.

The last bit of Israel we saw was a wall panel on the corridor leading to the plane itself. Christian and Muslim pilgrims come and pray and go. Jews make 'aliya', which means they immigrate. Which is fine for them, but where is the recognition of the human worth of Palestinians who

BRINGING THE JEWISH
PEOPLE HOME

have lived in the land for generations?

Next year in Jerusalem?

IN CONCLUSION

Jerusalem, Israel and Palestine are fascinating, energising, deplorable and exhausting by turns. One thing they are not is dull!

A big hot potato is the Bible. It is used by Orthodox Israelis, by Christian Zionists and by Palestinian Liberation Theologians. I have written an essay "Israel and the Bible: an Investigation" in which I examine what the various books of the Bible say about the land and statehood. It will not come as a surprise that, once again, there are no easy answers!

The essay can be downloaded for free from the Links page of my website www.bibleinbrief.org.

I hope that this book will have encouraged you to continue reading and talking. Two useful online newspapers are Ha'aretz (Israeli) and Al Jazeera (Arab). Sabeel provides a weekly email giving suggestions for prayer.

You do not have to go to Israel and the Palestinian Territories as part of a pilgrimage group. You can go on your own, staying in monasteries or cheap hotels, travel by bus, train or sheroot (shared taxi). I have alway felt (except on one occasion in 1996) completely safe. Just make sure you take your passport with you. And a copy of the Lonely Planet guide or similar. But whether you go in a group, or with friends or family, or on your own, just GO!

APPENDICES

APPENDIX 1

THE ARMENIAN GENOCIDE

A shadow lies over Jerusalem, or more specifically over the Armenian quarter of Jerusalem. Armenia is the oldest Christian country in the world, turning Christian 10 years before the conversion of Constantine. The shadow is the Armenian Genocide. It started on 24th April 2015 when about 250 Armenians notables were taken from Constantinople to Ankara and most of them killed. This led to a widespread killing throughout the Ottoman Empire. (At that time Palestine was part of the Ottoman Empire). All male Armenians were shot. Women, children and the elderly were sent on death marches into the Syrian desert and were not given food or water. Entire village populations were burnt to death, or sent to sea in boats which were then capsized and the people drowned. Assyrian Christians and Ottoman Greeks were similarly targeted. In 1914 the Armenian population was probably about 1,700,000. In 1917 it was 284,157. During the Turkish-Armenian war of 1920 a further 60,000 to 98,000 Armenian civilians were killed.

There is a long and well-documented article on the Armenian Genocide in Wikipedia.

Here is part of a short sermon preached in the Syrian Orthodox Church, on the 100th anniversary of the Armenian genocide, when Christians in Iraq and Syria were (and are) facing another possible genocide.

> *"We remember our Christian brothers who are suffering - young and old, and and women, sick and handicapped, bishops, priests, sisters and lay people mainly in our homelands of Syria and Iraq. Their endless tragedy and deprivation is neglected not only by their evil enemies of their true faith but even by some fellow brothers in the same faith.*

We also commemorate the centennial of 'saifo' or collective genocide of hundreds of thousands of our brothers who perished at the hands of evils who refuse the other.
Those who survived, resurrected from under the rubble more resilient, defeating evil with stronger faith and true partners of Christ's suffering and resurrection..."

When Hitler was asked if he was concerned about the stain which the extermination of Jews would have on his reputation, he replied, "Who remembers the Armenians?"

Tragically, little has changed.

.

APPENDIX 2

A DAY IN THE POLITICS OF ISRAEL

WHAT THE PAPERS SAID ON 30th JANUARY 2017

Newspapers were scarce in Jerusalem. In the departure lounge of Ben Gurion airport I finally got hold of the two main Israeli newspapers, Ha'aretz and the Jerusalem Post.

Ha'aretz is the oldest Jewish newspaper in the Holy Land, having started in 1918. Its title means "The Land". It takes a left-liberal stance. It has teamed up with the New York Times to be sold together with it.
The Jerusalem Post started in 1932 as the Palestine Post and changed its name in 1950. In the 1980's it became quite right-wing; it now has a more centrist position.

Here are the front page news stories for Monday 30th January:

New bill lets settlements seize Palestinian land
Knesset to vote today. Mendelblit (the attorney general) says he won't defend this version in court either.
The Knesset is scheduled to vote today on a revised "regularization bill" aimed at seizing private Palestinian land where settlement homes have been built, "innocently or at the state's instruction".

(Ha'aretz)

Knesset set to pass historic settlement legislation today
Bill would authorize 4,000 West Bank homes on private Palestinian property.
In a historic move, the Knesset is likely to pass into law the "settlement regularization bill" which retroactively legalizes close to 4,000 settler homes on private Palestinian property in Area C of the West Bank (where Israel has full control).
Netanyahu said, "The law is designed to normalise the status

143

of Jewish settlement in Judea and Samaria once and for all and prevent recurrent attempts to harm the settlement enterprise." (Jerusalem Post)

Will the ICC (International Criminal Court) take action?
The main question is ... what consequences Israel faces, specially with the International Criminal Court.... Sources close to Mandleblit say (this) amounts to suicide.
(Jerusalem Post)

Knesset mulls harsh law for illegal building
Bill goes to committee as pro-equality NGOs warn of its discriminatory effect on Israeli Arabs.
The bill's proposal to expand demolition of illegally-built homes ignores the state's long-standing failure to make adequate provision for legal construction in Arab towns, "which has led many people to break the law." (Ha'aretz)

Global backlash grows against Trump's immigration order
France, Germany, UK: Move is discriminatory. Order restricted by more US judges (Jerusalem Post)

Legal US residents fear travel under ban
An official said this includes green card holders, who are legal permanent US residents.
(Jerusalem Post)

Israelis born in Muslim countries may be blocked by U.S. travel ban
"We are waiting for the details and ramifications for Israeli citizens before deciding hat our next move will be", said a spokesman. (Ha'aretz)

Israel backtracks on EU program excluding settlements
The EU program, called Creative Europe, involves co-operation between EU and non-EU countries in the areas of culture and media. The significance of the proposal is that the government would in effect be agreeing to a boycott of the

settlements in the West Bank, East Jerusalem and the Golan Heights. (Ha'aretz)

Mexican Jews alarmed by Netanyahu tweet on Trump's wall

Donors suspend contributions to Keren Hayesod (the official fund-raising organisation for Israel).
Foreign ministry clarifies stance Netanyahu was not trying to intervene in the dispute. (Jerusalem Post)

Adding insult to injury: Trump flirts with classic Holocaust denial
The Trump administration's lame excuse for not mentioning Jews on Holocaust Remembrance Day on Friday falls into the category of "Yes, but" excuses (Ha'aretz)

Knesset panel approves release of 2014 Gaza war report

The report is expected to be a political bombshell for Netanyahu.
According to leaked portions of the report, the comptroller first slams the Prime Minister, the defence minister and the IDF chief of staff for failing to warn the security cabinet about intelligence they had received from Shin Bet (Israel Security Agency). The cabinet were told that there were overwhelming indications that Hamas was not prepared to go to war. Even when the war started, the three reportedly kept most of the key decisions and details to themselves, not sharing information with the security cabinet. (Jerusalem Post)

Funeral of murdered mother and two young sons draws hundreds

Hundreds of people attended the joint funeral of Dor Karsenti-Sela, 23, and her sons, 22 months and 8 months. Nadav Sela, 28, the husband and father was taken into custody. Nahman Attia, 11, who was visiting the family was also killed. Dor's mother said she was a devoted wife, letting him learn full-time in the yeshiva while she cared for the children.

(Ha'aretz)

And on the inside pages:

'Protecting children as individuals comes first'
Since the beginning of 2017, eight children have already been murdered by a parent, four children by their mother in Jerusalem, one child by a mother in Acre, and now three children in Migdal. "The past two years have been relatively quiet. I pray and hope that this is unequivocally not a rising trend." (Jerusalem Post)

Soldiers kill Palestinian attacker during violent clashes in Jenin
The army shot and killed a Palestinian after clashes broke out during an overnight raid in the Jenin refugee camp on Sunday. According to the IDF, Palestinians threw pipe bombs and stones at soldiers, who responded by firing toward the main instigators. No soldiers were wounded. Muhammad Mahmoud Abu Khalifa, 16, was killed and five others were wounded in the camp.
Last week, five members of Abu Khalifa's extended family, suspected of being Hamas members, were taken into custody during an IDF arrest raid in the same camp.
(Jerusalem Post)

19-year-old man killed by IDF in Jenin refugee camp during arrest operation
A 19-year-old Palestinian man was killed overnight Saturday and three others wounded during clashes with Israeli soldiers. Jenin residents said that Abu Halifa was the 23rd resident of the northern West Bank city to be killed since security incidents began to intensify in October 2015. "You have to remember that most of the youths are unemployed and have no framework, so they can hang about until the wee hours in the streets and alleys, and any entrance by an Israeli military vehicle could lead to a confrontation." (Ha'aretz)

Jerusalem strike fills street with garbage
A strike began Sunday morning in Jerusalem over the city's basic municipal services, including garbage collection, street cleaning and municipal offices....Jerusalem Mayor Nir Barkat is demanding the treasury give special grants to Jerusalem.

(Jerusalem Post)

Ploughing into the defenceless
The IDF officer asked his subordinates to help him with settlers harassing Palestinians. They ignored him.
An Israeli Defence Forces soldier ignored his commander's request to help him and four other soldiers overpower three settlers. The settlers had violated a military order by entering Palestinian land to disrupt plowing work.

(Ha'aretz)

Report: Israel enlarges W. Bank areas it's remapping in land-grab bid Israel has enlarged the territories it is remapping in the West Bank with the aim of declaring them state lands. The aim is to confirm that land now designated state land is indeed land over which Israel has legal jurisdiction, so it can build or expand settlements on it.   (Ha'aretz)

Haredi leaders demand repeal of Kotel resolution
The heads of the haredi political parties, the chief rabbis and the No.2 Agriculture Minister called on the prime minister to repeal the cabinet resolution calling for state-recognised progressive prayer area at the southern Western Wall. It is incompatible with the stance of the Chief Rabbinate.

The High Court indicated that it sees the current ban on women reading from a Torah scroll in the women's section of the main Western Wall plaza as problematic.   (Jerusalem Post)

And from the New York Times - front page

Who fears non-violence in Israel?

Issa Amro, a native of the city of Hebron and a prominent Palestinian advocate of nonviolent resistance, has been waiting now for nearly two months to find out when he can expect to face trial in an Israeli military courtroom. He has been accused of a series of offenses ranging from demonstrating without a permit to "insulting a soldier"...

Cruel absurdities are a commonplace of life in the occupied territories, but nowhere are they quite as intense as in Hebron. In the center of this city of some 200,000 Palestinians, a group of 800 Israeli settlers occupies heavily fortified positions, guarded by 650 Israeli soldiers. To manage this inherently combustible situation, the Israeli military has turned swathes of the central city into "sterile zones" in which Palestinians are no longer allowed to drive.

APPENDIX 3

A BLAST FROM THE PAST

ANDY'S VISIT IN 1990

At the end of April I paid my third visit to Israel. I had been there in 1963 and 1975 and so was able to compare Israel today with what it was like before.

Jerusalem is a very different place from what it was in 1975. Israeli soldiers are everywhere and have a very oppressive influence. It is very clear that three-quarters of the Old City is under foreign military occupation. Just inside the Damascus gate, in the heart of the Muslim quarter, where Palestinian Muslims have lived for centuries, is a house with a gigantic "menorah" (Jewish candelabra) on top and three soldiers permanently on duty. This is the house of Ariel Sharon, the hard-line former Minister of Defence, who was partly responsible for the massacre in the Palestinian refugee camps in Lebanon in 1983.

In my first week there, I took part in a protest by all church leaders against the occupation by Jewish settlers of a large hospice (70 rooms) right next to the Church of the Holy Sepulchre, part of the movement to make Jerusalem an all-Jewish city. (Israelis can live anywhere in Jerusalem, but by a High Court decision Palestinians are not allowed to live in the Jewish quarter). For the first time in its history, the Church of the Holy Sepulchre closed its doors, as did all but one of the other churches; even the Dome of the Rock closed its doors to tourists in solidarity. The really scandalous aspect of this unlawful occupation is that it was surreptitiously funded by Israel's Housing Ministry, via a company registered in Panama. Only a small minority of Israelis would support the settlers' action, but the internal splits in Israeli society make it impossible for Israelis who want to live in peace with Palestinians to respond effectively.

Some facts to put the present situation in perspective:

1948 - Fighting between Jews and Palestinians (e.g. Palestinians of

Tiberias were expelled before the British left). Terrorist acts on both sides; leading Jewish terrorists were Begin and Shamir.

- Israel declared independence, with the support of U.S.S.R. and U.S.A. Attacked by Egypt, Jordan and Syria. Great expansion of territory but loss of Old City of Jerusalem. 450 Arab villages destroyed and population expelled. 97,000 Arabs from Jaffa expelled in what Ben Gurion, first Prime Minister of Israel, called "a shameful and distressing sight". Creation of refugee camps in Jordan and Gaza Strip. West bank of Palestine annexed by Jordan.

1950's 600,000 non-Jews, mostly from N. Africa and Middle east, settled in Israel. Great improvement in the land with irrigation, re-afforestation etc. Movement of Israeli Arabs within Israel is rigidly controlled.

1967 - 6-day War. Israel captures Jerusalem, West Bank, Gaza Strip, Golan Heights. Arab countries refuse peace in exchange for recognition of Israel and return of captured territories. Arab villages near Tel Aviv-Jerusalem road and on Golan heights destroyed.

1982 - Invasion of Lebanon culminating in acquiescence to the massacres in Sabra and Chatila Palestinian refugee camps by Lebanese Christian militia with tacit Israeli support. Eventual forced withdrawal.

December 1987 - Start of "Intifada" - a spontaneous rejection by Palestinians in West Bank and Gaza of Israel's military rule.

1990 - Possible immigration of 250,000 Soviet Jews. Israeli pressure on U.S.A. to block possible immigration of Soviet Jews to U.S.A. Population now:

Israelis	3.7 million
Arabs in Israel proper	.7 million
Arabs in occupied territories	1.5 million

A key question is land. There are many laws by which Palestinian land can be taken over by the Israeli government. "State Land" which had the same status as our "common land" was taken for Israeli development. Land can be confiscated for "public purposes", and the

High Court has ruled that that includes confiscating privately owned Palestinian land to build houses for Jewish immigrants. If for some reason (e.g.drought) a field is not cultivated for five years, it can be confiscated. The compensation for confiscation used to be completely inadequate. Now it is more realistic, but only 4-5% of the land in Israel proper now remains in Palestinian ownership. In the West Bank 36% of the land has been acquired by Israel, and in Gaza 52%.

Since the Intifada started 20 Israelis have been killed and 250 injured. On the other hand the army has killed 823 Palestinians, seriously wounded 80,000, and destroyed 10,000 hones as collective punishment. One item I saw in the Jerusalem Post was of to young Palestinians painting graffiti at 4.15 a.m. Some soldiers discovered them and when they ran way shot one of them dead. This was, it was said, in line with the army's "open fire regulations".

I was told that over the last two years thousands of Palestinians have been arrested and jailed without charge for various periods. I met a Palestinian family on the Mount of Olives. Soldiers had broken down the front door at 2 a.m. one night and taken away the two younger teenage boys. They were detained without charge for three months, beaten and kept in a cupboard during interrogation. The saddest thing about it for me was the look of hatred in the eyes of the younger boy.

A Palestinian human rights worker was arrested, beaten in the police van and again in the police cell. He persevered in making a formal complaint, and eventually Yitzhak Rabin, the Defence Minister, replied to inquires by Jimmy Carter's Human Rights Committee. Rabin replied, "He was given only a moderate beating, enough to make him accept detention."

The situation can be summed up by the wife of Fritz (now Perez) Levinger, an old friend of my father's, who came to Palestine in 1933. She is a Jewish Israeli, and says that the attitude of Israelis towards Palestinians is now the same as German anti-Semitism against the Jews in the 1930's. While I was there, rabbi Moshe Levinger was sentenced for killing an Arab. In protest at stones thrown at his car, he had walked down a street in Hebron, shooting at random, walked into a shop and shot the shopkeeper through the head. He got 5 months.

So, what hope is there for peace?

The Intifada created the possibility of peace. For the first time there was a Palestinian leadership with whom Israel could have talked. The Intifada put considerable pressure on the P.L.O. outside Israel to come up with negotiations based on the real situation. The tragedy is that Israel has been unable to react except negatively. This is in line with the thoughts of the average Israeli. From the people I have talked to, especially young soldiers, taxi drivers etc., came the following thought process:

1. We want peace.
2. We would be prepared to exchange land for peace (but not Jerusalem).
3. But you can't trust Arabs.
4. To let Arabs have their land back would damage our security.
5. So we have to be strong.
6. So we cannot give any land back.
7. So, no peace.

In 1968 Moshe Dayan, the well-known Israeli general and politician, said:
"We are doomed to live in a constant state of war with the Arabs and there is no escape from sacrifice and bloodshed. This is perhaps an undesirable situation, but it is a fact. If we are to proceed with our work against the wishes of the Arabs, we shall have to expect such sacrifices."

SINCE 1990

Events in Israel and the Palestinian territories move fast. Nobody in 1990 could have predicted what the next 27 years would bring. Here is a brief account of the main events:

1993   The Oslo Accords, which planned for Israel to hand over control of the occupied territories in stages. Rabin said on the White House lawn: "We are two peoples destined to live in the same land."

1994   Arafat comes to Gaza to establish the new Palestinian Authority.

1995   In November Rabin assassinated by a right-wing Orthodox Israeli.

1996   Start of Hamas-inspired bombings and suicide bombings in Israel.

1999   Failure of negotiations between Barak and Arafat.
       Second Intifada sparked by Sharon's visit to the Temple Mount.

2001   Sharon Prime Minister. He occupied Gaza and West Bank towns.
       In the course of the Second Intifada, 2000 - 2005, more than 1,000 Israelis were killed, 70% civilians, and about 4,700 Palestinians were killed, of whom 43% were civilians

2004   Death of Arafat

2005   Sharon withdraws from Gaza and four settlements on the West Bank, and starts the Separation Fence around and inside the West Bank.

2006   Hamas defeats Fatah in parliamentary elections. Takes over Gaza by force.
       Second Lebanese war ends with a ceasefire agreement.

2007   Blockade of Gaza (to present)

2008   Major attack on Gaza (Operation Cast Lead) to halt missile attacks on southern Israel. 1,397 Palestinians and 5 Israeli soldiers were killed.

2014   Hamas-Israel 2-month war. 2,100 Palestinians and 73 Israelis killed, 17,200 home destroyed.

APPENDIX 4

THE ZIONIST NARRATIVE
as displayed at Ben Gurion Airport
with comments

As I went through security at Ben Gurion airport, I thought, well, that is the end of my Israel experience. How wrong I was! Going down to the departure lounge is a hundred yards long sloping corridor. All along one wall is a series of 22 large panels telling in words and pictures the Zionist story of Israel. Here is the text of the panels. I have added some of my own comments, because, as I said elsewhere, everything in Israel has at least two narratives. My comments are in italics.

There are two things I noticed in this Zionist narrative. One is how Palestinians are completely airbrushed out of the picture. They are not mentioned once. For Zionists, they simply do not exist. Whereas in fact, for better or worse, they do.

The other thing I noticed is what I can only call "chutzpah". "Chutzpah" is a Hebrew word whose closest English equivalent is "cheek". A good example is the Jew who murdered his parents, and at his trial threw himself on the mercy of the court on the grounds that he was an orphan.

120 YEARS OF ZIONISM

The first Zionist Congress was convened by Theodor Herzl in Basel, Switzerland in August 1897, 120 years ago. For the first time, Jews from around the world gathered to work towards the establishment of a national home for the Jewish people.

The term "National Home" or "Heimstätte" was coined by one of Herzl's associates Max Nordau in 1897, to avoid worrying the Ottoman authorities. "To us it signified "Judenstaat" (Jewish State) then, and it signifies the same now."

The yearning to return to Zion existed throughout all the years of exile. During the 19th century, it was reflected in the philosophies of the "Forerunners of Zionism" and the Hibat Tzion ("Lovers of Zion") movement. However, Herzl's vision for a Jewish state and his political activities to achieve that goal sparked a Zionist revolution within the Jewish world and "The age-old hope to return to the land of our fathers" began to be realized!

"At the time Herzl died, Zionism had become an established movement, yet it expressed a minority view in the Jewish world. Until the First World War all branches of Judaism were generally opposed to secular Zionism." ("Israel" - Rabbi Dr Dan Cohn-Sherbok, p. 150)

The World Zionist Organization was established at the first Zionist Congress in order to fulfill the national goals of the Jewish people and to lead the Zionist movement.

In this exhibition the World Zionist Organizaion presents the main activities of the Zionist movement during the 120 years of its existence.

Establishing the state of Israel, returning to Zion, reviving the Hebrew language and culture and settling the land are remarkable achievements of the Zionist movement!
However, the goals of Zionism have not yet been fully realized. Therefore the WZO and its branches and institutions continue to work in a variety of ways, both in Israel and abroad.

Herzl's vision continues to be a source of inspiration, in keeping with his words, "Zionism is an infinite ideal."

THE "STATE IN THE MAKING"

HERZL AND THE JEWISH STATE

Theodor Herzl (1860-1904) was the first statesman of the Jewish people in modern times.

In his book, The Jewish State, he conceived a plan to establish a state for the Jewish people. He renewed the sense of Jewish sovereignty and transformed Zionism into a recognized political entity throughout the world, starting the Jewish nation on its march towards statehood.

Is nationalism always a good thing? The history of Europe in the 20th century would suggest not.

THE ZIONIST CONGRESS

The first Zionist Congress in Basel, convened by Herzl in August 1897, formulated the "Basel Program" as its official platform: "Zionism seeks to establish a homeland, guaranteed by public law, for the nation of Israel in the land of Israel."

THE "STATE IN THE MAKING"

The first Zionist Congress established the World Zionist Organization, and later, the institutions of the "State in the Making". Herzl wrote in his diary, "At Basel I founded the Jewish state... Perhaps in five years, certainly in fifty, everyone will recognize this."

In 1912 the "Agudat Israel"was formed to unite ultra-orthodox rabbis and laity against Zionism. Zionism was viewed as a satanic conspiracy against God's will and equated with pseudo-messianism. Spokesmen declared that Zionism sought to leave religion out of the national life - as a result the Jewish state would betray the ideals of the Jewish heritage. In 1924 Jacob Israel de Han, a member of the executive of Agudat, was assassinated in Jerusalem by the Haganah. (Israel - Rabbi Dr Dan Cohn-Sherbok, p. 136)

THE BALFOUR DECLARATION
Herzl's efforts to gain international support for the establishment of the Jewish state were continued by successive Zionist leaders. Their great achievement was the "Balfour declaration" in 1917, in which the British government declared its support for the establishment of a national home for the Jewish people in the land of Israel.

In 1919 Balfour wrote: "In Palestine we do not propose even to go through the form of asking what the (wishes of the present inhabitants of the country) are. The four great powers are committed to Zionism and Zionism, be it right or wrong, good or bad, is rooted in age-long traditions, in present needs, in future hopes, of far profounder import than the desires and prejudices of the 700,000 Arabs who now inhabit this ancient land."
At this time the Jewish population of Palestine was 10% of the total, roughly the same number as Christian Arabs.

UN RESOLUTION ON THE 29th OF NOVEMBER
Political efforts continued at the same time as the development of the Jewish community in Israel. The decisive turning point was the UN resolution of November 29, 1947 which approved the end of the British mandate and the establishment of a Jewish state in Israel.
Other UN resolutions were:
2546 11 December 1969
Expresses its grave concern at the continuing report of violation of human rights in the territories occupied by Israel,
Condemns such policies and practices as collective and area punishment, the destruction of homes and the deportation of the inhabitants of the territories occupied by Israel;
Urgently calls upon the Government of Israel to desist forthwith from its reported repressive practices and policies towards the civilian population in the occupied territories and to comply with its obligations under the Geneva Convention relative to the Protection of Civilian Persons in Time of War

3092   7 December 1973

Expresses its grave concern at the violation by Israel of the Geneva Convention relative to the Protection of Civilian Persons in Time of War, of 12 August 1949, as well as the other applicable international conventions and resolutions, in particular the following violations:

a) The annexation of certain parts of the occupied territories;

b) The establishment of Israeli settlements in the occupied territories and the transfer of an alien population thereto;

c) The destruction and demolition of Arab houses, quarters, villages and towns;

d) The confiscation and expropriation of Arab property in the occupied territories and all other transactions for the acquisition of land between the Government of Israel, Israeli institutions and Israeli nationals on the one hand, and the inhabitants or institutions of the occupied territories on the other;

e) The evacuation, deportation, expulsion, displacement and transfer of the Arab inhabitants of the Arab territories occupied by Israel since 1967, and the denial of their right to return to their homes and property;

f) Administrative detention and ill-treatment inflicted on the Arab inhabitants;

g) The pillaging of archaeological and cultural property in the occupied territories;

h) The interference with religious freedom, religious practices and family rights and customs;

i) The illegal exploitation of the natural wealth resources and population of the occupied territories;

66/225   29 March 2012 - extracts

Expressing its grave concern about the extensive destruction by Israel, the occupying Power, of agricultural land and orchards in the Occupied Palestinian Territory, including the uprooting of a vast number of fruit-bearing trees and the destruction of farms and greenhouses, and the grave environmental and economic impact in this regard,

Expressing its concern about the widespread destruction caused by Israel, the occupying Power, to vital infrastructure, including water pipelines and sewage networks, in the Occupied Palestinian Territory, in particular in the Gaza Strip in the recent period, which, inter alia, pollutes the environment and negatively affects the water supply and other natural resources of the Palestinian people,

...

Aware of the detrimental impact of the Israeli settlements on Palestinian and other Arab natural resources, especially as a result of the confiscation of land and the forced diversion of water resources, and of the dire socioeconomic consequences in this regard,

Aware also of the detrimental impact on Palestinian natural resources being caused by the unlawful construction of the wall by Israel, the occupying Power, in the Occupied Palestinian Territory, including in and around East Jerusalem, and of its grave effect as well on the economic and social conditions of the Palestinian people,

Reaffirming the need for the resumption and accelerated advancement of negotiations within the Middle East peace process, on the basis of Security Council resolutions 242, 338, 425, 1397 etc....

Noting the Israeli withdrawal from within the Gaza Strip and parts of the northern West Bank and the importance of the dismantlement of settlements therein in the context of the road map, and calling in this regard for respect of the road map obligation upon Israel to freeze settlement activity, including so-called "natural growth", and to dismantle all settlement outposts erected since March 2001,

Stressing the need for respect and preservation of the territorial unity, contiguity and integrity of all of the Occupied Palestinian Territory, including East Jerusalem,

Recalling the need to end all acts of violence, including acts of terror, provocation, incitement and destruction,

Taking note of the note by the Secretary-General transmitting the report prepared by the Economic and Social Commission for Western Asia on the economic and social repercussions of the Israeli occupation on the living conditions of the Palestinian people in the Occupied Palestinian Territory, including East Jerusalem, and of the Arab population in the occupied Syrian Golan,

(the Assembly...)

1. Reaffirms the inalienable rights of the Palestinian people and of the population of the occupied Syrian Golan over their natural resources, including land, water and energy resources;

2. Demands that Israel, the occupying Power, cease the exploitation, damage, cause of loss or depletion, and endangerment of the natural resources in the Occupied Palestinian Territory, including East Jerusalem, and in the occupied Syrian Golan;

…

4. Stresses that the wall and settlements being constructed by Israel in the Occupied Palestinian Territory, including in and around East Jerusalem, are contrary to international law and are seriously depriving the Palestinian people of their natural resources, and calls in this regard for full compliance with the legal obligations affirmed in the 9 July 2004 advisory opinion of the International Court of Justice …

5. Calls upon Israel, the occupying Power, to comply strictly with its obligations under international law, including international humanitarian law, with respect to the alteration of the character and status of the Occupied Palestinian Territory, including East Jerusalem;

6. Also calls upon Israel, the occupying Power, to cease all actions harming the environment, including the dumping of all kinds of waste materials in the Occupied Palestinian

Territory, including East Jerusalem, and in the occupied Syrian Golan, which gravely threaten their natural resources, namely water and land resources, and which pose an environmental, sanitation and health threat to the civilian populations;

7. Further calls upon Israel to cease its destruction of vital infrastructure, including water pipelines and sewage networks, which, internally, has a negative impact on the natural resources of the Palestinian people;

STATE OF ISRAEL

Fifty years after the Basel Congress, Herzl's prophecy came true and on May 14th, 1948, David Ben-Gurion, who became the first prime minister, declared the establishment of the State of Israel.

If the State of Israel was created in accordance with a UN resolution, perhaps it should heed other UN resolutions.

SETTLEMENT & AGRICULTURAL DEVELOPMENT

Settling the country was the practical expression of the Zionist vision of establishing a state in the historic Jewish homeland. The settlement enterprise sought to implement the democratic values of a model society based on equality, brotherhood and mutual responsibility. The kibbutzim and moshavim are unique socio-economic models which exemplify these value.

AGRICULTURAL SETTLEMENT

The World Zionist Organization, through the Keren Kayemeth LeIsrael/Jewish National Fund (KKF/JNF) purchased land for settlement at the full market price. Villages, settlements, kibbutzim and moshavim, were established on these lands and in all regions of the country were filled with Jews returning to their land. These settlements developed diverse branches of agriculture and transformed a land deficient in water and natural resources into a flourishing "Land of Milk and Honey".

Much of the land of Palestine was under absentee ownership. Zionists would pay the absentee owners, living perhaps in Constantinople, and the local Palestinian farmers were then driven out.

I heard the Israeli deputy ambassador speak at the Sutton synagogue. He spoke strongly against the excessive government support given to the farming lobby, for instance in the large-scale production and export of oranges. "We're exporting water!" he lamented.

URBAN SETTLEMENT

At the same time, cities were built and development towns and community settlements were established. In the urban centers, crafts, industry, trade, science and technology grew and reached an international level.

In 1947 there were three urban centres with a considerable number of Jews: Tel Aviv, Jerusalem and Haifa

PERIPHERAL AND BORDER REGIONS

The settlements were established in outlying areas in order to diffuse the population as widely as possible and to protect Israel's borders. The distribution of the settlements created and continues to form the basis of the country's geographical boundaries.

This gives the Zionist blessing to all the internationally illegal settlements on the West Bank and Golan Heights. Settler controlled land now makes up 42% of the West Bank, including all the fertile Jordan valley. Again, see the UN resolution quoted earlier.

The last sentence above ("The distribution of the settlements...) seems a perfect example of "chutzpah", especially as in October 2011 UNESCO admitted the State of Palestine as a member, and in November 2012 the United Nations voted to upgrade the status of the Palestinians to that of a non-member observer state

CREATIVITY AND INNOVATION

Settlement members, in cooperation with researchers and academics, have produced remarkable achievements in Israeli agriculture such as water-saving irrigation, wastewater purification, seawater desalinization, development of new agricultural species, cultivation techniques and innovative agricultural machinery.

Israeli experts export the innovations of Israeli agriculture and assist in agricultural development throughout the world, especially in developing countries.

But not in the Palestinian territories?

THE REVIVAL OF THE HEBREW LANGUAGE AND CULTURE

The revival of the Hebrew language is a tremendous Zionist achievement! As a sacred language throughout the centuries of exile, Hebrew had been used mainly for study and prayer. Starting at the beginning of the 20th century, with the active encouragement of the Zionist movement, Hebrew was transformed into a living, spoken and modern language that became the official language of the State of Israel.

ELIEZER BEN YEHUDA
The journalist, Eliezer Ben Yehuda, worked diligently to revive the Hebrew language. To promote spoken Hebrew, he founded the Hebrew Language Committee, produced Hebrew newspapers, created new words to suit modern life and wrote a comprehensive and historical dictionary of the Hebrew language.

He brought up his son Ben-Zion to know nothing but Hebrew so as a child he had no friends. The family were also ostracised by the ultra-orthodox community for using Hebrew as an everyday language. Ben-Avi, as he later called himself, was an ardent advocate of a Latin-based script for Hebrew.

THE "WAR OF THE LANGUAGES"
In 1913, a public campaign was waged over the tendency to use German as the main language of instruction at the Haifa Technicon and the role of Hebrew in the educational system. This battle became known as the "War of the Languages". The victory of Hebrew symbolized the revival of the language as well as the national awakening.

LEARNING IN HEBREW
Kindergartens, school, institutes of higher education and teacher seminaries were established in which the language of instruction was Hebrew. Even in the world of traditional Talmudic study, many academies (yeshivot) were established that carried out studies in Hebrew.

HEBREW CULTURE

Hebrew culture began to flourish in all areas: literature and poetry, theater and film, music and dance, journalism and radio, television and the internet.

ONE NATION - ONE LANGUAGE

Hebrew unites the citizens of Israel from all ethnic communities and plays a major role in absorbing immigrants. The WZO maintains its Hebrew study programs in the Diaspora in order to strengthen the relationship between all segments of the Jewish people in Israel and in the Diaspora in order to strengthen the relationship among all segments of the Jewish people in Israel and in the Diaspora. Its Hebrew language instruction programs for potential immigrants help ease their absorption when they make Aliyah.

JERUSALEM

Jerusalem has been the eternal capital of the Jewish people since King David and was home to the Temple. Jerusalem is a symbol of the yearning of the Jewish people to return to its country.

JERUSALEM EXPANDS BEYOND ITS WALLS
For years, residents of Jerusalem lived only within the walls of the Old City. Starting in 1860, new neighbourhoods were built outside the walls of the Old City and by the end of the 19th century, Jews made up the majority of the city's population. The new neighbourhoods grew and expanded following the waves of Aliyah during the 20th century.

CAPITAL OF THE "STATE IN THE MAKING"
During the British Mandate, the World Zionist Organization established the National Institutions building in Jerusalem and the Hebrew University of Jerusalem. In effect, Jerusalem became the capital of the "State in the Making".

CAPITAL OF ISRAEL
During the War of Independence (1948), the Old City was taken by Jordan. After the founding of the state, Prime Minister David Ben-Gurion declared Jerusalem the capital of Israel and the Knesset officially confirmed: "With the establishment of the Jewish State, Jerusalem has once again become its capital."

Jerusalem was designated as home to the Knesset, the government ministries, the Supreme Court, the residences of the president and prime minister, the Chief Rabbinate and the Rabbinical High Court.

The international community do not recognise Jerusalem as the capital pending a final peace agreement and all their embassies are inTel Aviv.

MOUNT HERZL

In August 1949, Herzl's remains were brought for burial in Jerusalem, in accordance with his will and the decision of the Israeli Knesset. Since then, Mount Herzl has served as a national memorial, housing a burial plot for national leaders, a military cemetery, and the Yad Vashem Holocaust memorial center.

A UNITED JERUSALEM

During the Six Days War (1967), the city was unified once again. It grew rapidly and became the largest city in Israel. Mixed and varied populations live in Jerusalem and there is complete freedom of religion and worship for all.

There may be complete freedom of religion and worship. But Christians from Bethlehem cannot come to the Church of the Holy Sepulchre for worship without applying a week in advance for a permit, which they may or may not get. Palestinian women from the West Bank are not allowed in at all if they are widows or over 65. The "rapid growth" is made up largely of vast new settlements which make up a ring around Jerusalem on land captured in the Six Days War., all seen internationally as illegal. There is an unsaid policy of squeezing out the Palestinian inhabitants of East Jerusalem, through withdrawing residence permits, house demolitions and a network of regulations. Houses in the Muslim and Christian quarters of Jerusalem are increasingly being taken over by Jewish settlers. The High Court has decreed that Palestinian Arabs are not allowed to buy property in the Jewish Quarter. (What's mine is mine and what's yours is mine).

IMMIGRATION AND ABSORPTION

A PEOPLE RETURNS TO ITS LAND
Immigration to Israel ("Aliyah") is the fulfillment of the prophetic vision and a central value in the Zionist enterprise and Israel's Declaration of Independence.

There are about 15 million Jews worldwide. There are now 6.8 million Jews in Israel and the Occupied Territories.

THE YEARNING FOR ZION
Since the Babylonian exile, the yearning for Zion has occupied a central place in Jewish tradition and prayer. Yet, throughout two thousand years of exile, Jews have immigrated to Israel as individuals or in isolated groups.

THE WORLD ZIONIST ORGANIZATION PROMOTES ALIYAH
The World Zionist Organization viewed immigration to Israel as a prerequisite for the basis of a Jewish National Home. Thus, the WZO actively encouraged Aliyah throughout the years and continues to encourage Aliyah today.

This would be acceptable if it were not accompanied by constant and systemic attempts to make life for Palestinian Arabs as difficult as possible. For example, in a refugee camp in Bethlehem, Palestinians have to pay four times as much for their water as the neighbouring settlers, and in summer the water supply can be turned off for up to a month.

FROM SETTLEMENT TO STATE
The waves of Aliyah before and during the early years of the State doubled the population of the country and posed major challenges to both the leaders and the immigrants. At the same time, these waves of immigration brought Jews together from many countries and led to the creation of a multi-facetted and multi-cultural society.

Presumably this does not include the 700,000 Palestinians who were made refugees in 1948, nor the 300,00 who were made refugees in 1967.

YOUTH ALIYAH
The Zionist movement also developed unique frameworks for the immigration of young Jews including "Youth Aliyah"beginning in the 1930's and the "Naaleh" program ("Youth before Parents") from the 1990's.

ZIONIST DETERMINATION
Illegal deportation during the Mandate, as well as the waves of immigrants who arrived after the Six Days War from the Soviet Union, Ethiopia and Western countries, exemplify Zionist determination. Their Aliyah was rooted in the longing for Zion and the unbreakable bond between the Jewish people and its land.

THE CONTRIBUTION OF ALIYAH
Aliyah from various countries has strengthened the culture, education, economy and society of Israel and has demonstrated to the world Israel's national and moral commitment to all Jews of the Diaspora wherever they are.

And to no one else? Not to the stranger living in their midst?

MINORITIES

EQUAL RIGHTS
The Zionist movement sought to establish a model society in the Jewish state, where non-Jews, as well as Jews, would enjoy complete equal rights. In his book, The Jewish State, Herzl wrote: "If members of other faiths or of other nations reside among us, we will provide them with equal protection and rights under the law." In his utopian novel, Altneuland, Herzl detailed the way Arab residents would enjoy full political rights and would be fully integrated into the "New Society" in the country.

Utopian is right!

THE BALFOUR DECLARATION
The Zionist Congress adopted the Balfour Declaration (1917) which included the clause: Nothing shall be done which may prejudice the civil and religious rights of existing non-Jewish communities..." The Congress declared (1921), "We wish to live with the Arab people and together with them transform our common home into a flourishing community that ensures each nation undisturbed national development."

Balfour made it clear in other places he was not concerned in the slightest with "civil and religious rights of the non-Jewish communities", which made up 90% of the population!

THE DECLARATION OF INDEPENDENCE
Israel's Declaration of Independence called upon "the Arab inhabitants of the 'state of Israel ... to take part in the country, on the basis of full and equal citizenship and due representation in all it institutions, both temporary and permanent."

So why all the travel restrictions for 20 years, the confiscation of land, the nigh-impossibility of getting building permits etc.?

THE LAW OF CITIZENSHIP
The Law of Citizenship (1952) granted full citizenship to all residents of Israel. All minorities enjoy complete freedom of religion and worship, and are free to participate fully in the country's society, economy, culture, politics and legal system. Arabic is recognized as an official language of the country.

Not entirely true. Jews can only be married by orthodox rabbis. To do otherwise in Israel can bring a 2 year prison sentence. Marriages between members of different faith communities are illegal. However, citizens can go abroad to get married, and those marriages, including same-sex marriages, are recognised by the state. BUT if you are Jewish and have married abroad, you can only be divorced through the Israeli Orthodox Rabbinical Courts.

SHARED DESTINY
The Druze community established a Zionist Council, made a "Covenant of Brothers" and formed a partnership of shared destiny with Israel, Druze and Circassians serve in the IDF and reach senior ranks. Many Bedouins, as well, serve in the army.

And the 3 million Palestinian Arabs in Israel and the Occupied Territories? In a TV panel discussion in 2011, a rabbi, who made aliyah from New York five years before, said, "We will have to push them across into Jordan, and if they will not go, we will have to exterminate them."

DEFENCE AND SECURITY

THE FIRST DEFENCE FORCES
Herzl sought to establish a Jewish state by international agreement and in the spirit of peace. However, confronted by violent opposition by Arabs in the land, the young Jewish community set up defence forces: Bar Giora (1907), Hashomer (The Guild of Watchmen - 1909) and the Hagana (1920).

BRITISH ARMY RECRUITMENT
Many members of the Jewish community fought in the British Army as part of the Jewish Legion against the Turks in World War I or against the Nazis during World War II as members of the Palmach and the Jewish Brigade, which also helped to bring Holocaust survivors of the Land of Israel.

THE UNDERGROUNDS
When the British Government restricted Aliyah, limited the Jewish purchase of land and endangered the existence of the Jewish community during the 1930's and 1940's, underground defence forces were formed. The Hagana (Including the Palmach), the Irgun and the Lechi forces defended the Jewish community and acted against the Mandatory government, with the goal of establishing an independent state.

The Palmach were an elite fighting force. Following the UN Resolution, and particularly in January 1948 the quantity and cruelty of the mutual bloodshed of Jews and Arabs rose swiftly especially in Haifa and Jerusalem and around Jewish settlements in the Jordan valley (Sykes: Crossroads to Israel p.401) The Palmach went on killing sprees, blowing up houses and levelling villages. For instance, after 47 Jews had been killed at the Haifa oil refinery, the Palmach attacked Balad al-Sheikh, Haifa. Several dozen houses were destroyed and 60 villagers left for dead. After 1948 the Palmach with the Haganah became part of the IDF.

Lechi, or Lehi, otherwise known as the Stern Gang, was a Zionist paramilitary organisation. In 1940 Stern negotiated with Mussolini to establish Jewish sovereignty over Palestine, promising to come under the aegis of Italian fascism. He also proposed making a wartime alliance with Hitler, helping to transfer Jews from Europe to Palestine, and offering sabotage and espionage operations against the British   The offer was delivered to Berlin in January 1941, but there was no response. On 6th November 1944 two members of the Stern Gang murdered Lord Moyne, the British Minister in the Middle East in Cairo. From 1946 they sent bombs in the mail to British politicians, as well as bombing the British embassy in Rome. In September 1948 members of the Stern Gang, assassinated the United Nations envoy who was trying to arrange an international agreement on the status of Jerusalem. After this the Israeli government declared Lehi a terrorist organisation and arrested 200 members. In February 1949, four months later, they were all released as part of an amnesty. One of their leaders was Yitzhak Shamir, prime minster 1983-1984 and 1986-1992.

In July 1946 the Irgun, led by Menachem Begin, destroyed the south wing of the King David Hotel, the British military headquarters, killing 91 people, mostly civilians. An earlier attempt by Irgun to blow up the hotel was foiled when the Haganah told the British of the threat.

In December 1947 the Irgun rolled an oil barrel filled with explosives and metal bolts in front of Arab workers queuing for a bus outside the Damascus Gate. 15 were killed and 47 wounded.
Between 9th and 11th April 1948 between 100 and 120 Arabs were killed by Irgun and Lehi fighters at the village of Deir Yassin. So appalled was the Jewish commander in Jerusalem, David Shaltiel, that he wanted all the Irgun and Lehi fighters shot.

In all, the Irgun carried out 70 terrorist attacks 1938 - 1948.

On the other hand, Muslim groups, led by the soft-spoken, dignified, ruthless and anti-semitic Grand Mufti, Haj Amin, instigated violent and bloody riots against Jews, and the murder of moderate Palestinian leaders whom he saw as traitors. He encouraged the attack on the Jewish comunity in Hebron in 1929, when 60 Jews were murdered, the remaining 600 were only saved because of the bravery of one young British officer, since his Arab police force refused to intervene. Haj Amin helped instigate the Palestinain Revolt of 1936-1939. He was forced to flee arrest in 1937, and eventually reached Berlin where he worked for the Nazis by broadcasting and by recruiting Bosnian Muslims for the Waffen SS.

THE IDF
With Israel's formation, the defence forces were merged into the Israel Defense Forces (IDF). The State of Israel has not yet achieved regional peace and is forced to fight for its existence and protect its citizens. Conflicts in the region continue to cast a shadow on the security of Israel's citizens, despite peace agreements with Egypt and Jordan.
In addition to maintaining security, the IDF is a melting pot for immigrants and members of various ethnic communities. It also provides a framework for soldiers to complete their formal education and cultivates a sense of civic responsibility.

Chutzpah? The rise of domestic violence in Israel is often linked to the brutalising effect of the occupation on Israeli society.

The IDF frequently carries out rescue and relief operations for communities throughout the world at times of natural disaster.

They also man roadblocks and checkpoints in the West Bank. In September 2013 there were 99 fixed checkpoints and 174 surprise "flying checkpoints". The IDF's Judge Advocate General, Maj Gen Dr M Finkelstein stated that "there were many - too many - complaints that soldiers manning checkpoints abuse and humiliate Palestinians and the large number of complaints 'lit a red light' for him".

My wife accompanied a frail 70 year old English woman to an interrogation by a female Israeli soldier, when this inoffensive woman had forgotten her passport. The woman soldier was quite harsh. It was the male soldier who interceded for her, saying she should be allowed to sit down.

Kirstein-Keshet of Machsom (Checkpoint) Watch reports, "We Watchers... have witnessed the daily humiliations and abuse, the despair and impotence of Palestinians at checkpoints."

Ometz LeSarev (Courage to Refuse) is an organisation of reserve officers and soldiers of the IDF who refuse to serve beyond the 1967 borders. It started with 51 officers putting an open letter in Ha'aretz in January 2000. Three years later their number reached 300. This is part of the open letter:

"We, reserve combat officers and soldiers of the Israel Defense Forces ... who have always served in the front lines..

"We, who understand now that the price of Occupation is the loss of the IDF's human character and the corruption of the entire Israeli society...

"We shall not continue to fight beyond the 1967 borders in order to dominate, expel, starve and humiliate an entire people...

"We hereby declare that we shall continue serving in the Israel Defense Forces, in any mission that serves Israel's defense.

The missions of occupation and oppression do not serve this purpose - and we shall take no part in them."

TECHNOLOGICAL DEVELOPMENT AND CIVIL DEFENSE
The need to improve state security has led to the growth of an innovative technological industry, including civilian applications that have advanced technology worldwide, Israel has also become a world leader in cyber security.

WOMEN BREAK NEW GROUND

THE RIGHT TO VOTE FOR WOMEN
The Zionist Movement was one of the first national movements in history to give women the right to vote. Starting with the elections to the Zionist Congress in 1898, women enjoyed the right to vote and to be elected to public office. By comparison, women's suffrage was introduced in England only in 1918, in the United States in 1920 and in France in 1944.

PARTNERSHIP AND LEADERSHIP
Since the first waves of immigration, women have been fully integrated into the activities and leadership of the Zionist enterprise. Female kindergarten and elementary school teachers and educators played a central role in reviving the Hebrew language. The Young Women's Farm near the Sea of Galilee trained women in farming, and female pioneers worked alongside their male counterparts in agricultural work.

Partnership and equality within the Zionist movement enabled the young Golda Meir to assume leadership roles in the pre-state Jewish community. Later, with the establishment of the State, she was elected Minister of Labor, then Minister of Foreign Affairs and ultimately, Prime Minister of Israel.

WOMEN'S ORGANIZATIONS
Starting in 1911, women founded dynamic organizations in order to expand their roles in society and ensure their full participation in the development of the country. Charismatic women founded the Hadassah Oranization, WIZO, Na'amat, Emunah and Youth Aliyah.

WOMEN IN DEFENCE
Women served alongside men in the early security and defense forces, Hashomer, Hagana, Palmach, Irgun and Lechi. Today, women serve in the Israel Defense Forces in a variety of roles, including combat positions.

The Israeli novel, "The People of Forever are not Afraid" tells of three young women friends and their varied experiences in the IDF. "Shani Boianjiu lays bare for us what these young people must endure and the emotional collapse that often follows. She is able to replicate for us the almost paranoid mind-set the soldier must develop in order to survive and the scars it leaves on their psyches." (Jewish Journal)

PROMINENT WOMEN'S LEADERSHIP

Women have risen to prominence in key areas - the Knesset and the government, the judicial system, local government, the civil and foreign service, banks, large companies and the media.

Women's creativity in all fields of culture and the arts has enhanced the spiritual and intellectual character of Israeli society.

Female scientists contribute to the enrichment of science and research in Israel and abroad, and they have won prestigious awards, including the Nobel Prize.

A darker reality is that welfare officials in Israel estimate that there are 200,000 battered women and 600,00 children living with violence. The Knesset Speaker said in 2014, "Despite well-developed legal measures implemented to prevent violence against women, a tacit tolerance of the phenomenon fosters further attacks." 19 women were killed in 2013, and 10 in 2014.

During the 2015 summer's 50 day conflict with Hamas, police in southern Israel reported a dramatic spike in the number of domestic violence complaints. According to Ha'aretz the family violence hotline received 60% more calls during July 2014 than a month earlier. Police attributed this to the high-stress environment and the sustained amount of time the couples spent in fortified rooms.

But domestic violence against Palestinian women living in Israel is equally rife. In 2016 8 Palestinian women and 7 Israeli

178

women were killed in domestic violence. "What makes it a terrible situation for the Arab women is that there is no serious effort put in to stop these crimes and to stop the escalation happening."

ISRAEL AND THE DIASPORA

ONE NATION - ONE HEART
Zionism seeks to gather Jews from around the world together in Israel, where they will live in safety and contribute to Israel's development. However, the reality is that many Jews have remained in the Diaspora, where they have established Jewish communities and integrated into their surrounding societies economically, socially, culturally, and politically. Yet, despite the geographical distance, there is a great feeling of connection between Diaspora Jews and Israel. This relationship creates unity, a sense of identity and mutual responsibility.

Currently there are 6,400,000 Jews in Israel and between 7,800,000 and 9,500,000 in the rest of the world, by far the majority in the USA.
What I find particularly striking is that there are just over 6 million Jews in Israel and roughly 6 million Jews in North America, while 6 million were killed in the Holocaust.

There are 4,800,000 Palestinians in the West Bank and Gaza, 1,658,000 Israeli Arabs and about 3 million Palestinians living in Jordan. There are also 85,000 Palestinians living in USA, 630,000 in Syria, 500,000 in Chile,and 402,000 in Lebanon etc. (Wikipedia) i.e. there are over 6 million Arab Palestinians in Israel and the West Bank, not counting the 3 million in Jordan.

DIASPORA ASSISTANCE TO ISRAEL
Diaspora Jews helped to establish the State of Israel and assist in its development in many ways: appeals, donations to national and local projects, political support, public expressions of solidarity and mobilization of volunteers for civil and military service. Israel serves as a destination for tourists and family visits.

ISRAELI ASSISTANCE TO THE DIASPORA

The State of Israel views itself as responsible for the fate of Jewish people worldwide and assists them in every way possible. The national institutions sends educational emissaries to Jewish communities, provide them with relevant educational material to strengthen their knowledge of Judaism, conduct educational programs which promote Jewish and Zionist identity, and provide religious services.

STREAMS OF JUDAISM

Diaspora Jewry has developed liberal religious streams, which play an important role in Diaspora communities. Their influence has had a considerable impact on Israeli society as well.

Orthodox Jews account for 26.5% of Israelis and 27% of American Jews.

COMBATTING ANTI-SEMITISM

Anti-Semitism in increasing worldwide and is demonstrated by openly anti-Israel expressions and activities, as well as boycotts against Israel (BDS). The World Zionist Organization operates a communications center to combat these incidents and conducts diversified operations against them, in cooperation with Diaspora Jewry.

AN INFINITE IDEAL

I once called Zionism an infinite ideal... as it will not cease to be an ideal even after we attain our land, the Land of Israel. For Zionism... encompasses not only the hope of a legally secured homeland for our people... but also the aspiration to reach moral and spiritual perfection.

(Theodor Herzl, Our Hope,March 1904)

A MODEL STATE

Herzl sought to establish a model state for the Jewish people in the land of Israel, characterized by an enlightened, tolerant and progressive society. The new society in this country would be able to integrate Jewish and universal ideals, advance science and technology for the benefit of the entire world and strive to realize the unique ethos of "an infinite ideal".

A JEWISH AND DEMOCRATIC STATE

The Zionist movement established the State of Israel as a Jewish and democratic state, which also aspired towards a just society, focuses on the preservation and progress of the Jewish people, and strengthens the Jewish identity and the bond between Israel and the Diaspora. Israeli society is tasked with creating a true sense of connection among all of its ethnic, religious and cultural segments, based on respect, harmony, peace and equality. This is what Herzl called the "moral and spiritual perfection" of society.

It is impossible for Israel to take over the territories it has conquered and have a democracy, for then there would not be a Jewish majority. It can only be Jewish and democratic in the long term if it embraces the 2-state solution, which the settlments policy has made virtually impossible.

THE DESIRE FOR PEACE

The highest aspiration, combining all the hopes of the Jewish people since the dawn of history has been the inner peace of each individual, peace within our community and peace with our neighbours near and far.

In his last speech to the World Zionist Congress in December 1946, Dr Chaim Weizmann said:

"I warn you against bogus palliatives, against short cuts, against false prophets, against facile generalisations, against distortion of historic facts. If you think of bringing the redemption nearer by un-Jewish methods, if you lose faith in hard work and better days, then you commit idolatry and endanger what we have built. Would that I had a tongue of flame, the strength of prophets, to warn you against the paths of Babylon and Egypt. "Zion shall be redeemed in Judgement" - and by no other means."

APPENDIX 5

WHAT I MISSED IN JERUSALEM

There is so much to see in Jerusalem. Here are most of the places I would like to have seen if I had had time.

OLD CITY
Via Dolorosa, especially on a Friday
The Citadel/Tower of David & Museum
Arab Orthodox Women's Museum, David Street, Jaffa Gate
Western Wall Tunnels
Burnt House & Synagogues

OUTSIDE THE WALLS
Kidron Valley/Hezekiah's Tunnel

MOUNT OF OLIVES
Bethany (now cut off from the rest of the Mount by the Separation Wall).
Dominus Flevit Church
Tombs of the Prophets

EAST JERUSALEM
The Garden Tomb
Rockefeller Museum

WEST JERUSALEM
Bible Lands Museum
Mea Shearim
Islamic Museum
Museum on the Seam

FURTHER OUT
Ein Kerem
The Chagall windows in the synagogue of the Hadasseh Hospital near Ein Kerem.

Note: I visited Yad Vashem, the museum about the Holocaust, in 1995 and 2015. Extremely well done and sobering. In 1995 I was surprised that more visitors did not make the connection between the Nazi setting up of the Warsaw Ghetto and the current treatment of Palestinians.

APPENDIX 6

RECOMMENDED BOOKS AND FILMS

There are vast number of books and films on Israel and the Palestinians. Here are a few which I have found both enjoyable and helpful:

BOOKS

Lonely Planet Guise of Israel and the Palestinian Territories
an excellent guide book with information about all aspects of the region, historical, religious, political, gastronomic etc.

O Jerusalem   L Collins & D Lapierre
a dramatic account of the 1948 war, seen from both sides.

A War Without Chocolate   Betty Majaj
The life story of a Lebanese Christian woman and her family living in Jerusalem from 1947

The Lemon Tree   Sandy Tolan
Two families whose lives form a microcosm of half a century of Israeli-Palestinian history

Blood Brothers   Elias Chacour & David Hazard
a Palestinian Christian and priest works for peace in Israel

The Palestinian-Israeli Conflict: a Very Short Introduction
                    Martin Bunton

Jerusalem - the Biography   Simon Sebag Montefiore
3,000 years of history, reads like a thriller

FILMS

Seven Broken Cameras

A Palestinian farmer bought a video camera to record his fourth son's life from birth, just as Israeli settlers started to build a fence round their village. This is not fiction! It is a home movie about what life is like for Palestinians on the West Bank over 5 years. Essential viewing.

Death in Gaza

A documentary about life in the Gaza Strip. It was to have been paired with a documentary about Israelis living under the threat of Hamas rockets, but the film-maker was killed by an Israeli sniper first.

Paradise Now

A drama of two young Palestinians recruited to be suicide bombers. Wonderful, non-violent, thought-provoking film.

Cup Final

A 1992 film of two Israeli soldiers captured by Palestinian fighters in the Lebanon war. It turns out they all support Manchester United! (It does not end well for the Palestinians).
Sadly now virtually unobtainable except as VHS

Waltzing with Bashir

A powerful documentary about an Israeli soldier's experience of the Lebanese war.

The Green Prince

A quite astonishing documentary of how the son of a Hamas leader became an informer for Shin Bet.

Lightning Source UK Ltd.
Milton Keynes UK
UKOW07f0314121017
310856UK00007B/58/P